# Essentia

## of **Psychological Assessment** Series

Everything you need to know to administer, score,
and interpret the major psychological tests.

**I'd like to order the following** *Essentials of Psychological Assessment:*

- ❑ WAIS®-III Assessment / 0471-28295-2
- ❑ WJ III™ Cognitive Abilities Assessment / 0471-34466-4
- ❑ Cross-Battery Assessment, Second Edition / 0471-75771-3
- ❑ Nonverbal Assessment / 0471-38318-X
- ❑ PAI® Assessment / 0471-08463-8
- ❑ CAS Assessment / 0471-29015-7
- ❑ MMPI-2™ Assessment / 0471-34533-4
- ❑ Myers-Briggs Type Indicator® Assessment / 0471-33239-9
- ❑ Rorschach® Assessment / 0471-33146-5
- ❑ Millon™ Inventories Assessment, Second Edition / 0471-21891-X
- ❑ TAT and Other Storytelling Techniques / 0471-39469-6
- ❑ MMPI-A™ Assessment / 0471-39815-2
- ❑ NEPSY® Assessment / 0471-32690-9
- ❑ Neuropsychological Assessment / 0471-40522-1
- ❑ WJ III™ Tests of Achievement Assessment / 0471-33059-0
- ❑ WMS®-III Assessment / 0471-38080-6
- ❑ Behavioral Assessment / 0471-35367-1
- ❑ Forensic Psychological Assessment / 0471-33186-4
- ❑ Bayley Scales of Infant Development II Assessment / 0471-32651-8
- ❑ Career Interest Assessment / 0471-35365-5
- ❑ WPPSI™-III Assessment / 0471-28895-0
- ❑ 16PF® Assessment / 0471-23424-9
- ❑ Assessment Report Writing / 0471-39487-4
- ❑ Stanford-Binet Intelligence Scales (SB5) Assessment / 0471-22404-9
- ❑ WISC®-IV Assessment / 0471-47691-9
- ❑ KABC-II Assessment / 0471-66733-1
- ❑ WIAT®-II and KTEA-II Assessment / 0471-70706-6
- ❑ Processing Assessment / 0471-71925-0
- ❑ School Neuropsychological Assessment / 0471-78372-2
- ❑ Cognitive Assessment with KAIT
  & Other Kaufman Measures / 0471-38317-1
- ❑ Assessment with Brief Intelligence Tests / 0471-26412-1

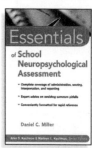

**Please complete the order form on the back.**
**To order by phone, call toll free 1-877-762-2974**
**To order online: www.wiley.com/essentials**
**To order by mail: refer to order form on next page**

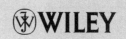

# Essentials

## of **Psychological Assessment** Series

# ORDER FORM

Please send this order form with your payment (credit card or check) to:
John Wiley & Sons, Attn: J. Knott, 111 River Street, Hoboken, NJ 07030-5774

NAME _____

AFFILIATION _____

ADDRESS _____

CITY/STATE/ZIP _____

TELEPHONE _____

EMAIL _____

❏ Please add me to your e-mailing list

Quantity of Book(s) ordered _____ x $34.95$^*$ each

| Shipping Charges: | Surface | 2-Day | 1-Day |
|---|---|---|---|
| First item | $5.00 | $10.50 | $17.50 |
| Each additional item | $3.00 | $3.00 | $4.00 |

For orders greater than 15 items, please contact Customer Care at 1-877-762-2974.

**PAYMENT METHOD:**

❏ Check/Money Order    ❏ Visa    ❏ Mastercard    ❏ AmEx

Card Number _____ Exp. Date _____

Cardholder Name *(Please print)* _____

Signature _____

*Make checks payable to **John Wiley & Sons**. Credit card orders invalid if not signed.*
*All orders subject to credit approval. * Prices subject to change.*

To order by phone, call toll free 1-877-762-2974
To order online: www.wiley.com/essentials

# Essentials of Assessment with Brief Intelligence Tests

# Essentials of Psychological Assessment Series

Series Editors, Alan S. Kaufman and Nadeen L. Kaufman

# Essentials

## of Assessment with

## Brief Intelligence Tests

Susan R. Homack

Cecil R. Reynolds

 John Wiley & Sons, Inc.

# CONTENTS

# SERIES PREFACE

In the *Essentials of Psychological Assessment* series, we have attempted to provide the reader with books that will deliver key practical information in the most efficient and accessible style. The series features instruments in a variety of domains, such as cognition, personality, education, and neuropsychology. For the experienced clinician, books in the series will offer a concise yet thorough way to master utilization of the continuously evolving supply of new and revised instruments, as well as a convenient method for keeping up to date on the tried-and-true measures. The novice will find here a prioritized assembly of all the information and-techniques that must be at one's fingertips to begin the complicated process of individual psychological diagnosis.

Wherever feasible, visual shortcuts to highlight key points are utilized alongside systematic, step-by-step guidelines. Chapters are focused and succinct. Topics are targeted for an easy understanding of the essentials of administration, scoring, interpretation, and clinical application. Theory and research are continually woven into the fabric of each book but always to enhance clinical inference, never to sidetrack or overwhelm. We have long been advocates of what has been called intelligent testing—the notion that a profile of test scores is meaningless unless it is brought to life by the clinical observations and astute detective work of knowledgeable examiners. Test profiles must be used to make a difference in the child's or adult's life, or why bother to test? We want this series to help our readers become the best intelligent testers they can be.

The continually increasing demands on mental health services, as well as the time and financial constraints placed on assessment practices by the managed care community, often make a comprehensive intellectual assessment impractical. Information relating to general levels of intellectual function is useful to clinicians in a variety of circumstances wherein a comprehensive assessment of intellectual skills is unnecessary. In such cases, a reliable and valid estimate of global intelligence provided by a brief intelligence measure can be immensely helpful. In *Essentials of Assessment with Brief Intelligence Tests,* readers are provided with descriptions and interpretive information on four of the most widely used brief intelligence measures, also chosen for coverage herein according to a set of criteria related to quality and practicality of the instruments: the Kaufman Brief Intelligence Test, Second Edition (KBIT-2), the Reynolds Intellectual Screening Test (RIST), the Wechsler Abbreviated Scale of Intelligence (WASI) and the Wide Range Intelligence Test (WRIT). The foundation and application of each instrument are highlighted and specific instructions for administering, scoring, and interpreting each measure are proffered. Illustrative case examples and sample evaluations are provided to highlight the similarities and differences of each measure. Information necessary to select brief intelligence tests appropriate to the client's background, the clinician's need for information, and to administer and interpret brief intelligence measures with ease is provided. We trust that those who use intelligence tests in clinical and related (e.g., school) settings will find this coalescence of information in a single source useful in decision-making and in the interpretation of brief intelligence tests.

*Alan S. Kaufman, PhD, and Nadeen L. Kaufman, EdD, Series Editors*
Yale University School of Medicine

# Essentials of Assessment with Brief Intelligence Tests

# One

## INTRODUCTION AND OVERVIEW OF THE USES OF BRIEF INTELLIGENCE TESTS

This volume reviews the concept of brief intelligence testing and presents concise information on four brief intelligence tests that we consider the most salient to school and clinical practices. The volume as a whole follows the concise format of the Wiley Essentials series in so doing. This chapter provides an overview and definition of brief intelligence testing, as well as discussing its uses and limitations. Past efforts at developing short forms of tests and problems with such tests are noted as well. In subsequent chapters, we review information on the four brief intelligence tests we think most likely to meet the needs of a variety of clinicians and provide a chapter of sample evaluations that have used brief intelligence measures.

In choosing these tests, we used criteria that turned out to be highly similar to those of Kaufman and Lichtenberger (2006). Each of these four measures (in alphabetical order, as are the chapters devoted to them), the Kaufman Brief Intelligence Test, second edition (KBIT-2; Kaufman & Kaufman, 2004b), the Reynolds Intellectual Screening Test (RIST; Reynolds & Kamphaus, 2003a), the Wechsler Abbreviated Scale of Intelligence (WASI; Psychological Corporation, 1999), and the Wide Range Intelligence Test (WRIT; Glutting, Adams, & Sheslow, 2000, are relatively recent; have up-to-date, carefully selected norms; assess individuals across a wide age range; yield scores in verbal and nonverbal domains; produce scores with relatively good reliability evidence; present appropriate validity evidence for test score interpretation; and, for most examinees, require less than 30 minutes (this last requirement being questionably met for the WASI).

## WHAT IS A BRIEF INTELLIGENCE TEST?

Here we define a brief intelligence test as a rapidly administered test that provides information on global aspects of intelligence, but is relatively narrowly assessed. These tests do not provide sufficient breadth of coverage for application to clinical or educational diagnosis of cognitive disorders. *Brief* in our definition refers to both coverage and administration time. We did not, for example, include the Reynolds Intellectual Assessment Scales (RIAS; Reynolds & Kamphaus, 2003b) here, due to its breadth of coverage. Although typically administered to most examinees over 25 to 35 minutes, the subtests involve broad, complex mental processes, the reliabilities of the obtained scores are routinely above .90 (even at the subtest level), and it has a conormed memory scale (verbal and nonverbal) that can be added to the calculation of the various intellectual composite scores provided. Hence, it is as useful (and more so, in some cases) as much longer intelligence tests that purport to be more comprehensive (see especially Chapters 1 and 6 of Reynolds & Kamphaus, 2003b).

## WHAT ARE REASONABLE APPLICATIONS OF BRIEF INTELLIGENCE TESTS?

The question of why one would prefer a brief intelligence test over a more comprehensive measure is certainly salient and cogent. If it is important to measure intelligence, is it not important to measure it well?

Many brief intelligence tests do measure intelligence well, despite our admonition that they should not be used in diagnosis of cognitive disorders, if they meet our criteria noted in Rapid Reference 1.1. There are many times when knowledge of general levels of intellectual functioning ($g$) and levels of intellectual skills in the verbal and nonverbal domains are useful

---

≣ *Rapid Reference 1.1*

...........................................................................................................

## Characteristics of the Most Useful Brief Intelligence Tests

- Recent, up-to-date, population-proportionate standardization samples
- Allow assessment of a wide age range
- Provide scores with relatively good reliability (i.e., major scores with alpha coefficients above .80)
- Provide evidence to support the validity of test score interpretation
- Provide for at least measurement of general intelligence, or *g, and* verbal and nonverbal intellectual domains
- Should require less than 30 minutes of administration time for most examinees

but diagnosis of a cognitive disorder is not at issue. In the context of an evaluation of behavioral and emotional problems, for example, a comprehensive intellectual assessment will not always be useful. Rather, general knowledge of the individual's overall level of intelligence is sufficient to determine whether or not the behavioral or emotional problems are associated with lower levels of cognitive development. In the context of therapy, an estimate of global intelligence is useful because individuals at different overall levels of intelligence may benefit differentially from certain interventions. Brief IQ tests will not only be appropriate but also useful in any circumstances where a global estimate of general intelligence, or *g,* is all that is desired by the clinician. In the following we present and discuss what we view as the remaining principal applications of brief intelligence tests.

### Screening for More Comprehensive Evaluations

There are numerous times when it is desirable to locate as many people as possible who have a specified set of characteristics. To assess everyone in a population with a comprehensive measure quickly can become overwhelming and impractical, both financially and logically. Screening methods are often employed to sift through large groups and to determine, on a probability basis, who is most likely to have these characteristics. The use of objective test data in such decisions greatly reduces a host of referral biases (e.g., see Kamphaus & Frick, 2002). When a specified level of intelligence is one such characteristic, brief intelligence tests are useful in such a screening process.

Additionally, practitioners might use a brief intelligence measure in a public health clinic, pediatric practice, preschool or prekindergarten screening program (Reynolds, 1979), managed care organization, veterans hospital, or other setting to assess risk for functional intellectual impairment. The following are some specific examples of such situations as suggested by Reynolds and Kamphaus (2003b, p. 117) with a few additions of our own:

- A managed care organization uses a screener at intake for all mental health and elderly patients in order to rule out intellectual impairment.
- A child referred for ADHD is screened for intellectual problems because learning disability (LD) is known to be a relatively frequent comorbidity.
- A school district conducts a screening of all entering kindergarteners to rule out significant developmental delays.
- Prior to implementing Response to Intervention (RTI) methods in special education referrals, all referred children are administered a brief intelligence test to rule in or out the need for a comprehensive assessment for Mental Retardation.
- A psychologist screens all stroke/CVA patients prior to discharge from hospital-based rehabilitation to ensure that significant intellectual impairment is not present.
- A treatment center for patients with HIV screens advanced cases in order to determine whether intellectual impairment has occurred due to the advanced stage of the disease.

- A hospital screens all patients over age 75 years who are scheduled for surgery with a general anesthetic or other highly invasive procedure to determine cognitive level for understanding issues of consent and to establish an intellectual baseline.
- A hospital screens all major organ transplant patients pre- and postsurgery to evaluate potential cognitive impairments that may lead to comprehensive neuropsychological evaluations.
- A pediatric psychologist screens children subsequent to treatment with prophylactic chemotherapy for acute lymphocytic anemia to rule out cognitive sequelae.
- A program for intellectually gifted and talented children uses individual intelligence testing to screen applicants for possible admission into the program.

One might legitimately pose the question, why not just employ a group intelligence test in large-scale screening as opposed to a brief, individually administered intelligence test? There are actually many good reasons. Most group-administered intelligence tests, even very popular ones such as the Wonderlic Personnel Test (Wonderlic, 1999) and the Shipley Institute of Living Scale (Zachary, 1986) invoke reading as a principal medium of testing for intelligence. This creates a level of confounding between reading skill and measured IQ that is unacceptable in many circumstances. There are numerous examples in the media of exceptionally bright individuals who experience significant reading problems (of which even Albert Einstein has been purported to have suffered to some extent). Psychologists and other clinicians encounter this phenomenon frequently. A severe discrepancy between reading skill and measured IQ was the hallmark indicator of the presence of a learning disability for over 50 years and was even written into many state and federal laws (e.g., Reynolds, 1985).

There are certainly group-administered intelligence tests that are non-verbal—that do not rely on reading at all (e.g., the Beta III; Kellogg & Morton, 1999). However, such tests are frequently too narrow, ignoring the entire domain of verbal reasoning and other aspects of problem-solving in

> ### DON'T FORGET
>
> Group-administered tests have severe limitations in the screening of intellectual function.

> ### DON'T FORGET
>
> When screening for intellectual levels, evaluation of both verbal and nonverbal domains is necessary for most (not all) purposes.

> ### DON'T FORGET
>
> Verbal intelligence is nearly always found to be a superior predictor (versus nonverbal intelligence) of academic outcomes.

language-related domains. Nonverbal group measures of intelligence are useful principally when assessing individuals who have limited English proficiency, and are also helpful even with fluent speakers when English is a second language. However, even then, the purpose of the screening will dictate the applicability of nonverbal measures. Verbal intelligence is found routinely to be a better predictor of any form of academic success (when compared to nonverbal intelligence) whether school achievement, vocational training programs, or related work (e.g., see Kamphaus, 2001; Kaufman & Lichtenberger, 2006; and Sattler, 2001, for reviews).

There are several special purposes for which brief intelligence tests are particularly useful. These will be discussed in the following, but remember that many other circumstances exist (as noted previously). In a variety of these areas, group-administered tests are used; however, the use of brief, individually administered tests would in fact prove more accurate and hence more efficacious. Before discussing these areas, it is useful to discuss the issue of errors in screening.

### Errors in Screening with Brief IQ Tests

All procedures used for assessment, diagnosis, classification, and the like are, inevitably, sometimes wrong. The frequency and type of errors that are most likely to occur vary depending upon the setting of cutoff scores or the interpretation given to the outcome. When using brief IQ tests as screening measures (i.e., to reduce the total number of persons who need to undertake a more comprehensive examination or evaluation), there are two types of errors that can occur. One is a false positive error and the other is a false negative error. A classification matrix indicating these error types is given in Figure 1.1.

In this matrix, the hit rates or sensitivity and specificity of the screening procedure (here a brief IQ test) are evaluated against the outcome when using a comprehensive assessment as the ultimate criterion. *Sensitivity* is defined as the ability to detect the presence of something (here, most likely Mental Retardation, qualification for a program for the intellectually gifted, a job training program, etc.) when it is actually present. *Specificity* refers to the ability to detect the absence of something when it is in fact not

<table>
<tr><td></td><td colspan="2">Outcome of<br>Comprehensive<br>Assessment</td></tr>
<tr><td></td><td>Qualifies</td><td>Does Not<br>Qualify</td></tr>
<tr><td>Screening<br>Procedure<br>Indication — Qualifies</td><td>1<br>+ +</td><td>2<br>+ -</td></tr>
<tr><td>Does<br>Not<br>Qualify</td><td>3<br>- +</td><td>4<br>- -</td></tr>
</table>

Box 1: A true positive
Box 2: A false positive
Box 3: A false negative
Box 4: A true negative

Boxes 2 and 3 represent errors of classification by the screening measure.

**Figure 1.1  Illustration of classification outcomes for screening procedures with a comprehensive assessment as the criterion measure**

present. The sensitivity and specificity rates of any procedure are affected by cutoff scores, which affect false positive and false negative error rates. Typically, when we attempt to increase the sensitivity of our screening procedure, we increase the false positive error rate (we identify too many people who do not ultimately qualify) but our false negative rate decreases. When we attempt to increase the specificity of our procedure, the opposite effect is noted: The false negative rate increases (we eliminate too many people who would in fact qualify if given the comprehensive assessment), while the false positive rate decreases. However, changes in sensitivity and specificity are not directly or proportionately linked to one another—that is, if we increase sensitivity by 10 percent we may or may not decrease specificity by the same amount (10 percent). This inequality occurs because of the base rates of qualifiers—the mathematical explanation is beyond the scope of our work here. Suffice it to say that any time cutoff scores are set or changed, sensitivity, specificity, and our error matrix should be recalculated. (See Rapid Reference 1.2.)

Is it better to make more, less, or equivalent proportions of false positive or false negative errors? There is seldom a hard factual answer to this question in our field. The answer is always contextual and ultimately a policy decision. In some cases, the answer is clear. Suppose we were screening people for a correctable heart defect that if undetected was nearly always fatal. Here it is clear that we would tolerate a high false positive rate due to the dire consequences associated with false negative errors. However, suppose we are screening for admission to a school district's program for the intellectually gifted. We still want to have a small false negative error rate, but, given the cost of comprehensive evaluations, we might well tolerate a higher false negative error rate than in the case of our heart defect example. In choosing to use screening procedures, it is always a good idea to consider not just error rates, but the type of er-

### ≡ Rapid Reference 1.2

Sensitivity = the ability to detect something when it is present.

Specificity = the ability to detect the absence of something when it is absent.

ror that is most likely to occur and the consequences of each type of error.

> **DON'T FORGET**
> ........................................................
> When using screening procedures, do not consider just the overall error rate. Also consider the type of errors likely to be made: false positive and false negative.

Another way to view such errors is to calculate the positive and the negative predictive power of a brief test at different cutoff points. This is a way of restating error rates as probabilities. Positive predictive power is the probability that a person scoring at our above a particular cutoff point will qualify on the comprehensive evaluation. Negative predictive power is the probability that a person scoring below a particular cutoff point will not qualify on the comprehensive evaluation.

Remember in all cases that even comprehensive examinations and the lengthiest of tests also will misclassify a number of individuals. However, when choosing to use a screening measure, it is best to validate it and compute error rates against what will be the final criterion for qualification.

### Screening for Programs for the Intellectually Gifted

Schools often seek to identify and provide a variety of programmatic enrichments, specialized instruction, and academic advancement to students with high to very high IQ levels. Multiple methods are used to discover these students including teacher and parent nomination, group-administered tests of intelligence and achievement, and nomination by other school staff. These approaches, all totaled, can generate an overwhelming number of referrals while even missing students, especially those with behavior problems, limited English proficiency, or even reading disabilities—some of whom will undoubtedly have very high levels of intelligence. Various biases will also exist in subjective referrals. School districts vary in

> **DON'T FORGET**
> ........................................................
> All forms of psychological tests and measurements have associated error rates, not just brief tests or short forms.

setting cutoffs for participation in such programs, but IQs of 125 to 130 are common standards.

Many school districts (including several among the 10 largest in the United States) have opted to use brief intelligence tests, most commonly among the four detailed in this book (the KBIT-2 and the RIST being especially popular in this context), for this purpose. When used in this manner, cut scores that dictate a more comprehensive examination are quite different from the scores ultimately required to gain entrance into the program. As noted previously, when screening, one must consider the types of error that are most acceptable: false positive or false negative errors. In the case of screening for a program for the intellectually gifted, false positive errors are more desirable, since we do not want to deny inappropriately any student's participation in the program. A cut score that triggers continued referral and more comprehensive evaluation will then be set lower. For example, if the RIAS is used as the criterion measure of intelligence and the cutoff for admission to the program is a RIAS Composite IQ (CIX) of 125 and the RIST (which takes only 8 to 12 minutes per student to administer) is used as a preliminary screening measure, a RIST IQ cutoff of 118 or higher might be set for the screening instrument. This value is chosen based on actual data indicating that very few children who earn RIST IQs of 117 or less will earn a RIAS CIX of 125 or higher. It will still identify more students than will ultimately qualify (the false positive error rate), but it will disqualify very few students who would ultimately meet the criteria based on the more comprehensive testing (the false negative rate). Given the costs in time and in money, screening with brief IQ measures makes great sense in such circumstances.

### Screening for Programs for Cognitive Impairments

Public schools are charged under federal laws with identifying and serving all students with a disability. Cognitive impairments nearly always cause problems of an academic nature. Various processing disorders, traumatic brain injuries, illnesses of various sorts (and sometimes their treatments), as well as such well-known conditions as Mental Retardation and a host of genetic conditions (e.g., see Fletcher-Janzen & Reynolds, 2003; Goldstein & Reynolds, 1999) can result in cognitive impairments. It is quite expensive to administer individual tests to large numbers of students, so once again brief IQ tests come to mind, and are used to screen for a variety of cognitive problems. Some large school districts actually administer a brief IQ test (most of which we are aware use either the KBIT-2 or the RIST) to every incoming student, whether new to school or a transfer student.

### Screening for Vocational Programming or Employment Selection

Screening for vocational programming or employment selection both represent additional circumstances in which large numbers of individuals may need to be evaluated and when the use of group tests is questionable. Most brief IQ tests, and particularly the four we have chosen here, have relatively high correlations with academic outcomes, which means that they will do well in predicting who will be successful in completing vocational training programs with various levels of academic demands.

Additionally, many employers have established IQ-cutoff levels for certain positions within their companies or agencies (all in accordance with the regulations of the Equal Employment Opportunity Commission and the U.S. Office of Civil Rights). Police and other public safety agencies often set such cutoffs for intellectual levels, for example, as do many corporations when hiring at upper-level management and executive levels. Even brokerage and financial asset management companies often use IQ measures as one component of the hiring decision. In such circumstances, brief IQ measures are an efficient means of evaluation of intellectual function.

### Other Applications of Brief IQ Tests

While we are certain that there are additional applications we have not seen, there are also additional uses of brief IQ tests we have employed in our own practices and that have been suggested by other authors (e.g., Kaufman & Lichtenberger, 2006).

### Referrals Associated Primarily with Affective or Behavioral Disturbances

In 27 years of clinical practice, one of us (CRR) always found it useful to assess intellectual level as a necessary component of understanding emotional and behavioral problems. Kaufman and Lichtenberger (2006) also suggest that an IQ estimate is useful in psychiatric referrals. Psychiatrists routinely include an estimate of global intelligence as a component of the mental status examination of patients of all ages (although psychiatrists and other medical personnel are most likely to base this estimate on language usage, especially vocabulary, and little else; e.g., Sadock & Sadock, 2000).

The constraints of time available to psychologists working in public agencies, such as schools, the continually increasing demands on mental health services, as well as the time and financial constraints placed on assessment practices by the managed care community, often make a comprehensive intellectual assessment impractical or prohibitive in many such cases. A comprehensive assessment of intellectual functioning may well be unnecessary as well; however, a reliable and valid estimate of global intelligence and perhaps verbal and nonverbal intellectual skills can be immensely helpful. This is when brief IQ tests can be employed profitably.

Levels of intellectual development are important to understand when considering behavioral and emotional data, and in the interpretation of personality and behavioral test data. Several examples come to mind quickly. When interpreting various projective tests, for example, developmental level is crucial. Transparencies in human figure drawings are quite common by individuals prior to age 6 years. Beginning around age 6 years, such signs are pathognomic. However, this is related to cognitive development. Transparencies in a human figure drawing by a 7-year-old with an IQ of 125 would (or should) be inter-

## DON'T FORGET

Knowledge of general levels of intellectual functioning can improve your understanding and interpretation of emotional and behavioral problems.

preted quite differently than the same drawings produced by a 7-year-old with an IQ of 75.

The same may be true of behavioral data. It might very well be appropriate to interpret behavior-rating scale data on an instrument like the BASC-2 (Reynolds & Kamphaus, 2004) quite differently for children of the same age but with quite disparate levels of cognitive development. This would seem to be especially true of scales assessing such characteristics as attention and hyperactivity, when the culprit simply may be a low level of cognitive development overall and not something like Attention-Deficit/Hyperactivity Disorder (although the incidence of ADHD is higher among individuals with Mental Retardation than in the general population). Knowledge of cognitive development is important to understanding and interpreting adaptive behavior scales, as well. Individuals' levels of understanding of the complexities of their psychosocial and entire ecosystems will be important in evaluating affective and behavioral issues at all ages. Intellectual skills are important in providing a frame of reference for such interpretations.

### Making Treatment Recommendations in Emotional and Behavioral Referrals

Level of intellectual development globally and in the verbal and nonverbal domains can influence response to certain interventions. For example, individuals with average and higher intellectual levels are more likely to benefit from individual psychotherapy approaches, certain forms of group therapy, and bibliotherapy than are other individuals. Persons with below-average levels of intelligence are less likely to benefit from insight-oriented treatment approaches and behavioral interventions are more likely to be successful. Detailed knowledge of cognitive development often is not necessary in such circumstances, but valid, reliable knowledge of general levels of intellectual development is certainly useful.

### Research When IQ is Needed as a Covariate or Related Variable

In research projects in which intellectual level is needed to demonstrate group characteristics, for matching samples, or as a covariate in nonrandom samples, brief IQ tests are an efficacious alternative to comprehensive examinations (when IQ itself is not the focus of the research; in that case, a comprehensive measure is more likely to produce useful results). Brief IQ tests are nearly always superior to group IQ measures for reasons given earlier. King and King (1982) argued that research applications were in fact the most valuable applications of brief IQ tests. Kaufman and Lichtenberger (2006) disagree with this view—we do as well—and see brief IQ tests as important in all the domains noted previously. If forced to choose, perhaps it would be most efficient to use brief IQ tests in the assessment of referrals for emotional, behavioral, and related psychiatric problems.

## WHY NOT USE SHORT FORMS OF COMPREHENSIVE TESTS?

In the past, clinicians used short comprehensive forms of intelligence measures, such as the Wechsler intelligence scales, to assist in obtaining a brief estimate of intelligence. While using a shortened version of a Wechsler intelligence scale served as an acceptable means of estimating intelligence for decades, and the development of short forms of the Wechsler Scales became a cottage research industry of its own (Kaufman, 1990; Kaufman, Ishikuma, & Kaufman-Packer, 1991; Prifitera, Weiss, & Saklofske, 1998; Reynolds, Willson, & Clark, 1983; Silverstein, 1982), short forms exhibit some limitations that should be of concern for clinicians. First, clinicians have used too many alternative ways of shortening the Wechsler batteries. One common method of shortening a Wechsler battery is to use only a few items from each subtest (Satz & Mogel, 1962). Others have selected a few subtests based on psychometric properties, coverage of cognitive functioning, or testing time (Doppelt, 1956; Kaufman et al., 1991; Mc-Nemar, 1950; Reynolds et al., 1983; Silverstein, 1982). Regardless of how a clinician goes about shortening an intelligence measure, unnecessary time is spent attempting to develop what one hopes may be an adequate short form. Typically, short forms have altered the order of subtest administration or the item sequence. On measures like the Wechsler scales, on which autocorrelations exist across subtests by order of administration, this is problematic as research has indicated that individuals may perform differently on such short forms than on a full Wechsler instrument (Saklofske & Schwean-Kowalchuk, 1992; Sattler, 1988; Thompson, 1987). Subtest administration order, motivation, and fatigue may produce differential scores on short forms of comprehensive intelligence scales.

Smith, McCarthy, and Anderson (2000) reviewed in detail what they considered the seven sins of short-form development (i.e., reasons why reliability and validity are commonly overestimated). Kaufman and Lichtenberger (2006) also reviewed numerous problems with derivative short forms taken by abridgement of comprehensive scales. We are in essential concurrence that, when these problems with short forms exist, they should not be used.

Of the four brief IQ tests that are the subject of this work, only the RIST (Reynolds & Kamphaus, 2003a) is a derivative. It is included here because it does not have the problems of other derivative short forms as designated by Smith et al. (2000) and by Kaufman and Lichtenberger (2006), and due to its very brief administration time (8 to 12 minutes), strong reliability, and extensive validity data. The RIST is composed of the first two subtests of the RIAS (nullifying the issues of order effects and fatigue) and the item sequence is common as well. Extensive reliability and validity data are reported, it includes a verbal and nonverbal task, and, in general, meets all the criteria for a brief IQ test in Rapid Reference 1.1.

## SUMMARY

While brief intelligence tests should not be used for diagnosis of cognitive disorders, they are helpful in many circumstances in which a comprehensive intellectual assessment is unnecessary or impractical. Most often, this will be in various screening applications, but includes other uses, such as the assessment of individuals with emotional and behavioral disorders. Group tests that rely upon reading skills or ignore the verbal domain will be confounded as screening measures of overall intelligence, and are quite often too narrow to function without unacceptable rates of errors. Brief intelligence tests can provide objective, efficacious data that are consistently superior to subjective selection or referral methods.

## TEST YOURSELF

1. **Which of the following are characteristics of the most useful brief IQ tests? (Mark all that apply.) They**

   (a) are very inexpensive to purchase.

   (b) have recent and up-to-date normative samples.

   (c) are flexible (e.g., they allow examiners to choose items to match examinees).

   (d) are typically administered in 30 minutes or less.

   (e) are no more than two subtests in length.

   (f) are reliable measures of g and of verbal and nonverbal intelligence.

   (g) are presented with evidence of reliability and validity.

   (h) are useful for diagnosis of the most common cognitive disorders.

   (i) typically overestimate IQ levels so that no examinee is penalized for having taken a brief IQ test.

   (j) are most useful in research applications and not in a clinical setting.

2. **Sensitivity in assessment refers to**

   (a) the ability of the examiner to relate to the examinee.

   (b) the practice effects seen on retesting.

   (c) the ability of a test to detect the presence of something.

   (d) the ability of a test to detect the absence of something.

3. **Specificity in assessment refers to**

   (a) the ability of the examiner to relate to the examinee.

   (b) the practice effects seen on retesting.

   (c) the ability of a test to detect the presence of something.

   (d) the ability of a test to detect the absence of something.

**4. Which of the following is nearly always the best predictor of academic achievement?**

    (a) overall intelligence or g

    (b) nonverbal intelligence

    (c) verbal intelligence

    (d) mother's educational level

**5. Reading skill of the examinee is often a confounding factor in the use of**

    (a) group-administered intelligence tests.

    (b) comprehensive, individually administered intelligence tests.

    (c) brief, individually administered intelligence tests.

    (d) group-administered reading tests.

**6. False positive errors**

    (a) are the most common error made by brief IQ tests.

    (b) are the least common error made by brief IQ tests.

    (c) are the most serious type of error in all assessment conditions.

    (d) none of the above.

**7. False negative errors**

    (a) are the most common error made by brief IQ tests.

    (b) are the least common error made by brief IQ tests.

    (c) are the most serious type of error in all assessment conditions.

    (d) none of the above.

**8. In setting cutoff scores for screening measures, the most important factor to consider is**

    (a) the overall error rate.

    (b) false positive errors.

    (c) false negative errors.

    (d) the balance between false positive and false negative error rates in the context of the screening application.

(*continued*)

**9. When screening for intellectual level**

    (a) g is the only important concern.

    (b) verbal and nonverbal intelligence should be considered.

    (c) memory assessments should nearly always be considered.

    (d) working memory and processing speed are the best estimators in most cases.

**10. Brief IQ tests are useful in which of the following: (Mark all that apply.)**

    (a) Estimating IQ of psychiatric referrals.

    (b) Screening for programs for the intellectually gifted.

    (c) Screening for top-level management positions.

    (d) Diagnosing Mental Retardation.

    (e) Diagnosing various neurodevelopmental and genetic conditions.

    (f) Research on intelligence.

    (g) Research when intelligence is a crucial covariate.

*Answers:* 1. b, d, f, g; 2. c; 3. d; 4. c; 5. a; 6. d; 7. d; 8. d; 9. b; 10. a, b, c, g

Two

# KAUFMAN BRIEF INTELLIGENCE
# TEST–SECOND EDITION (KBIT-2)

The KBIT-2 is an individually administered intelligence test introduced in 2004 that is an update and substantial revision of the original KBIT (Kaufman & Kaufman, 1990). The KBIT-2 is a brief standardized measure of verbal (crystallized) and nonverbal (fluid) intelligence used to assess children, adolescents, and adults ages 4 through 90 years. According to the *KBIT-2 Manual* (Kaufman & Kaufman, 2004b), this measure is appropriate for screening high-risk individuals who will require subsequent in-depth evaluation, rechecking periodically the intellectual status of individuals who were previously administered a comprehensive evaluation, gifted and talented screening, obtaining vocational or rehabilitation information, research purposes, or when it is not possible to administer a full battery due to time constraints. According to the authors (Kaufman & Kaufman, 2004b), the KBIT-2 is not a substitute for a comprehensive measure of intelligence and users should not diagnose, place, or make neuropsychological interpretations based on obtained scores. Furthermore, a thorough evaluation should be recommended if the examinee's KBIT-2 standard scores or behavioral observations suggest the possibility of cognitive, educational, or emotional problems (Kaufman & Kaufman, 2004b).

Administration of the full KBIT-2 battery yields Verbal, Nonverbal, and IQ Composite scores. The three subtests of the KBIT-2 include Verbal Knowledge, Matrices, and Riddles. The Verbal Knowledge and Riddles

---

Portions of this chapter are adapted with permission of the copyright holder, American Guidance Service, Inc. from A. S. Kaufman & N. L. Kaufman (2004b), Kaufman Brief Intelligence Test–Second Edition, Circle Pine, MN: AGS Publishing.

## ≡ *Rapid Reference 2.1*

### KBIT-2 Subtests

| Subtest | Description | Measures |
|---|---|---|
| Verbal Knowledge | 60 items requiring the examinee to point to a picture that shows the meaning of a word or provides the answer to a question | receptive vocabulary, range of general information (nature, geography, the arts, science, etc.) |
| Riddles | 48 items requiring the examinee to either point to a picture that answers a riddle or say a single word that answers the riddle | verbal knowledge, reasoning, verbal comprehension |
| Matrices | 46 items requiring the examinee to point to a picture that best goes with a stimulus picture, completes an analogy, or solves a matrix | nonverbal reasoning, cognitive flexibility, problem-solving ability |

subtests compose the Verbal Scale and yield the Verbal standard score while the Matrices subtest makes up the Nonverbal Standard Score. The three subtests of the KBIT-2 that comprise the Verbal, Nonverbal, and IQ Composite scores take approximately 15 to 30 minutes to administer. Testing time tends to be shortest for young children and longest for adults. For a description of the three KBIT-2 subtests, see Rapid Reference 2.1.

Kaufman and Kaufman (2004b) had several goals in mind

## DON'T FORGET

The three subtests of the KBIT-2 that comprise the Verbal, Nonverbal, and IQ Composite score take approximately 15 to 30 minutes to administer.

when revising the original KBIT. The objectives of the KBIT revision were to enhance positive features of the original KBIT, correct any noted problems, and update norms. Due to concerns regarding the effects of reading and spelling abilities on the Definitions subtest of the KBIT, the revision of the KBIT focused on developing alternative means to measuring verbal ability. Test developers also sought to develop a test that could be easily administered by examiners with a wide range of training in assessment, including paraprofessionals. The one-word responses required for the KBIT-2 Riddles task and the multiple-choice format used for Verbal Knowledge and Matrices subtests lend themselves to easy administration and objective scoring.

## STANDARDIZATION AND PSYCHOMETRIC PROPERTIES OF THE KBIT-2

The standardization sample for the KBIT-2 ($N = 2{,}120$) was selected according to the March 2001 Current Population Survey, and was matched according to sex, race/ethnicity, geographic region, and educational level. Twenty-three age groups were created ranging from age 4 to 90, with 50 to 125 participants in each age group. Internal-consistency coefficients were computed for the Verbal, Nonverbal, and IQ Composite scores for each of the 23 age groups. Average reliability coefficients for the IQ Composite were quite impressive, ranging from .89 to .96 and averaging .93 across the entire age range. Split-half reliabilities for the Verbal score have high reliability both for children and adolescents aged 4 through 18 (mean = .91), and for adults aged 19 through 90 (mean = .92). Overall reliabilities for the Verbal score range from .86 to .96 (mean = .90). For the Nonverbal score, reliabilities are high both at ages 4 to 18 (mean = .86) and at ages 19 to 90 (mean = .91). While still acceptable, reliabilities of the Nonverbal score for the children ages 4 and 5 years are somewhat lower (mean = .78). Overall reliabilities range from .78 to .93 (mean = .88) for the Nonverbal score. Split-half reliabilities for the KBIT-2 normative sample by age are provided in Table 2.1.

**Table 2.1 Split-half reliability of the KBIT-2 normative sample by age**

| Age | Verbal | Nonverbal | IQ Composite |
|---|---|---|---|
| 04–18[a] | 0.90 | 0.86 | 0.92 |
| 19–90[a] | 0.92 | 0.91 | 0.95 |
| 04–90[a] | 0.91 | 0.88 | 0.93 |

Reliabilities for the Verbal score and IQ Composite were computed using the formula provided by Nunnaly (1978, p. 248).

[a]Weighted mean, using Fisher's $z$ transformation.

The test-retest method was used to assess the stability of scores on the KBIT-2. The KBIT-2 was administered twice to 271 children, adolescents, and adults aged 4 though 89. Testing was conducted within a period of 6 to 56 days with an average interval of 4 weeks. Demographic characteristics of the test-retest sample were divided into four age ranges. Retest reliabilities of the Verbal score ranged from .88 to .93 (mean = .91) while retest reliabilities ranged from .76 to .89 (mean = .83) for the Nonverbal score. Test-retest reliability of the IQ Composite ranged from .88 to .92 (mean = .90). Overall, there tended to be a slight practice effect of about 2 to 5 standard score points on the Verbal, Nonverbal, and IQ Composite scores. The average gain on the IQ Composite for all age groups was 4 points. See Table 2.2 for a list of test-retest reliabilities for the KBIT-2 by age.

Comparison studies investigated the relationship between the KBIT-2 and the *Wechsler Intelligence Scale for Children–Third Edition* (WISC-III; Wechsler, 1991) and *Fourth Edition* (WISC-IV; Wechsler, 2003), and the *Wechsler Adult Intelligence Scale–Third Edition* (WAIS-III; Wechsler, 1997). In two separate studies, the KBIT-2 was administered to children and adolescents along with either the WISC-III or WISC-IV. The KBIT-2 and WISC-III were administered to 43 children and adolescents ages 6 to 15 while the KBIT-2 and WISC-IV were administered to 63 children and adolescents ages 6 to 16. The KBIT-2 IQ Composite correlates .76 and .77 with the

## Table 2.2 Test-retest reliabilities for the KBIT-2 by age

| Ages | | Adjusted Correlations | |
| --- | --- | --- | --- |
| | Verbal | Nonverbal | IQ Composite |
| 4–12 | 0.88 | 0.76 | 0.88 |
| 13–21 | 0.93 | 0.80 | 0.89 |
| 22–59 | 0.89 | 0.89 | 0.92 |
| 60–89 | 0.92 | 0.85 | 0.92 |
| Mean | 0.91 | 0.83 | 0.90 |

All reliability coefficients were corrected for restriction of range based on the standard deviation obtained on the first testing, using the variability correction of Cohen et al. (2003, p. 58).

WISC-III and WISC-IV Full Scale IQ scores (FSIQ). The KBIT-2 IQ Composite correlates .84 with the WISC-IV General Ability Index (GAI), which is made up of the Verbal Comprehension and Perceptual Reasoning subtests. The KBIT-2 Verbal score correlates .83 and .79 with the Verbal IQ (VIQ) on the WISC-III and the Verbal Comprehension Index (VCI) on the WISC-IV. The KBIT-2 Nonverbal score correlates .53 and .56 with the WISC-III Performance IQ (PIQ) and the WISC-IV Perceptual Reasoning Index (PRI), indicating that the KBIT-2 does not seem to measure the same constructs as the WISC-III Performance IQ and WISC-IV Perceptual Reasoning Index. The KBIT-2 and WAIS-III were administered to 67 examinees aged 20 through 48. The correlation between the KBIT-2 IQ Composite and WAIS-III FSIQ was .89. Correlations between the KBIT-2 Verbal and WAIS-III VIQ is .81, while the KBIT-2 Nonverbal and WAIS-III PIQ correlation is .79. A correlation study with the *Kaufman Assessment Battery for Children–Second Edition* (Kaufman & Kaufman, 2004a) was not completed in time for inclusion in the manual; however, results will be posted on the Pearson Assessment Publishing website (www.pearson.com) upon study completion. Tables 2.3 and 2.4 provide lists of correlations between the KBIT-2 and the WISC-IV and WAIS-III.

**Table 2.3  Correlations between the KBIT-2 and the WISC-IV (ages 6–16)**

| | Adjusted Correlations KBIT-2 | | |
| --- | --- | --- | --- |
| | Verbal | Nonverbal | IQ Composite |
| WISC-IV | | | |
| Verbal Comprehension Index (VCI) | **0.79** | 0.52 | 0.82 |
| Perceptual Reasoning Index (PRI) | 0.38 | **0.56** | 0.62 |
| Working Memory Index (WMI) | 0.47 | 0.23 | 0.48 |
| Processing Speed Index (PSI) | 0.07 | 0.08 | 0.12 |
| Full Scale IQ (FSIQ) | 0.66 | 0.55 | **0.77** |
| General Ability Index (GAI)[a] | 0.73 | 0.65 | **0.84** |

*Note.* Numbers in bold print denote convergent correlations. These coefficients are predicted to be substantial because the scores being compared measure similar abilities.

All correlations were corrected for restriction of range, based on the standard deviation obtained on the KBIT-2, using the variability correction of Cohen et al. (2003, p. 58).

[a]Based on Vocabulary, Comprehension, Similarities, Block Design, Matrix Reasoning, and Picture Concepts (Raiford, Rolfus, Weiss, & Coalson, 2005).

The KBIT-2 was correlated with two other brief cognitive ability tests: the original KBIT and the *Wechsler Abbreviated Scale for Intelligence* (WASI; Psychological Corporation, 1999). The KBIT-2 and the original KBIT were administered to 181 individuals in three age ranges: 4 to 7 ($N = 54$), 8 to 14 ($N = 53$), and 16 to 45 ($N = 74$). Correlations between the KBIT-2 and KBIT IQ Composites ranged from .80 to .86. For all three age groups, the correlations between the Verbal subtests of the KBIT-2 and KBIT ranged from .77 to .84. The correlations for the Nonverbal portions of the two measures were more variable. For ages 8 to 14 and 16 to 45, correlations ranged from .78 to .79. At ages 4 to 7, the Nonverbal

**Table 2.4 Correlations between the KBIT-2 and the WAIS-III (ages 20–48)**

| | Adjusted Correlations KBIT-2 | | |
| | Verbal | Nonverbal | IQ Composite |
| --- | --- | --- | --- |
| WAIS-III | | | |
| Verbal IQ (VIQ) | **0.81** | 0.64 | 0.84 |
| Performance IQ (PIQ) | 0.66 | **0.79** | 0.83 |
| Full Scale IQ (FSIQ) | 0.79 | 0.75 | **0.89** |
| Verbal Comprehension Index (VCI) | **0.82** | 0.58 | 0.80 |
| Perceptual Organization Index (POI) | 0.61 | **0.83** | 0.82 |
| Working Memory Index (WMI) | 0.59 | 0.62 | 0.70 |
| Processing Speed Index (PSI) | 0.28 | 0.34 | 0.37 |

*Note.* Numbers in bold print denote convergent correlations. These coefficients are predicted to be substantial because the scores being compared measure similar abilities.

All correlations were corrected for restriction of range, based on the standard deviation obtained on the KBIT-2, using the variability correction of Cohen et al. (2003, p. 58).

subtests of the KBIT-2 and the KBIT correlated .47. The KBIT-2 and the WASI were administered to 142 examinees in two age ranges: 7 to 19 ($N = 80$) and 35 to 52 ($N = 62$). Correlations between the KBIT-2 IQ Composite and WASI Full Scale IQ (4 subtests version) are .81 and .90 for the younger and older age groups, respectively. The KBIT-2 Verbal score correlates with the WASI VIQ at .80 and .86 for younger and older age groups, respectively. The correlation of the KBIT-2 Nonverbal score and the WASI PIQ is .62 for the younger sample and .80 for the older sample.

To provide further evidence of convergent and discriminant validity of the KBIT-2, this measure was correlated with two achievement measures: the *Kaufman Test of Educational Achievement–Second Edition, Comprehensive Form* (KTEA-II; Kaufman & Kaufman, 2004c) and the *Wide Range Achievement Test–Third Edition* (WRAT-3; Wilkinson, 1993). The KBIT-2 and the KTEA-II Comprehensive Form were administered to 105 students aged 6 through 18. The KBIT-2 IQ Composite correlates .74 with the KTEA-II Comprehensive Achievement score. The KBIT-2 IQ Composite and Verbal score correlates higher with Reading and Oral Language (approximately .70) than with Mathematics and Written Language (approximately .60), while the KBIT-2 Nonverbal score correlates at about the same level with all four achievement areas (low .40s). The KBIT-2 and the WRAT-3 were administered to 79 students aged 7 to 19 years. The KBIT-2 IQ Composite correlates about .50 with the WRAT-3 Reading, Spelling, and Arithmetic scores. The KBIT-2 Verbal score correlates .65 with the WRAT-3 Reading and Spelling and .37 with Arithmetic, while the KBIT-2 Nonverbal score correlates .44 with Arithmetic, .17 with Reading, and .13 with Spelling.

The KBIT-2 Verbal and Nonverbal scales are intended to measure crystallized ability and fluid reasoning. Research in this area indicates a growth and decline of crystallized and fluid abilities with age (Kaufman & Lichtenberger, 2002). To learn more about whether the KBIT-2 trends are consistent with research, growth curves were calculated for each of the KBIT-2 subtests for individuals aged 4 to 90. According to Kaufman and Kaufman (2004c), mean raw scores on the Verbal Knowledge and Riddles subtests should increase steadily through early adulthood, peak during middle age, and then decline gradually. In contrast, mean raw scores for the Matrices subtest should peak earlier in adulthood and decline through the rest of adulthood. Consistent with previous research, average raw scores on the Verbal Knowledge and Riddles subtests increased steadily from age 4 through young adulthood, peaked at around age 30, maintained a consistent level until age 60, and then declined. In contrast, mean raw scores on the Matrices subtest increased during childhood and adolescence, peaked at age 18, and remained consistent until about age 40. According to Kaufman and Kaufman (2004b), decline after age 40 was significant: Mean performance at age 50 was equivalent to that at ages 14 and 15, and at age 60 the average raw scores were comparable to that of 11- to 12-year-olds. These results on age differentiation provide evidence of the construct validity of the KBIT-2.

## ADMINISTRATION AND SCORING POINTERS

In this section, we present important reminders for competent administration for each of the three subtests of the KBIT-2. To assist with the ease of administration, Kaufman and Kaufman (2004b) designed the subtests so that they have many common administration procedures and rules. For example, the basal and ceiling rules are the same for all three KBIT-2 subtests. While some of the scoring rules are consistent across the three subtests, administration rules for each subtest should be reviewed in detail. A review of the three KBIT-2 subtests and administration rules is provide in the following. (See Rapid Reference 2.2.)

### *Verbal Knowledge*

The Verbal Knowledge subtest is made up of two item types, one assessing the examinee's general information and the other measuring receptive vocabulary. On the Verbal Knowledge subtest, the examiner says a word or asks a question and the examinee points to the picture that best answers the question. Administration of the Verbal Knowledge subtest of the KBIT-2 requires the stimulus book and record form. The first page of the Verbal Knowledge section of the stimulus book provides the examiner with administration and scoring instructions. Directions to be read aloud to the examinee are provided in the record form. Verbal prompts for each item used by the examiner are printed in blue ink in the record form in

**DON'T FORGET**

Across the three KBIT-2 subtests, the basal rule is three consecutive correct responses and the ceiling is reached when the examinee responds incorrectly to 4 consecutive responses.

## ≡ *Rapid Reference 2.2*

### Kaufman Brief Intelligence Test–Second Edition (KBIT-2)

**Author:** Alan S. Kaufman & Nadeen L. Kaufman

**Publication date(s):** 2004

**What the test measures:** Verbal, nonverbal, and general intelligence

**Age range:** 4–90

**Administration time:** 15 to 30 minutes

**Qualification of examiners:** Graduate- or professional-level training in psychological assessment or technicians and paraprofessionals if trained by qualified personnel

**Publisher:** AGS Publishing
4201 Woodland Road
Circle Pines, MN 55014-1796
Ordering phone number: (800) 328-2560
http://www. agsnet.com

**Price** (as of May 2006): KBIT-2 Complete kit test price = $204.99

## DON'T FORGET

When administering the Verbal Knowledge subtest, verbal prompts are printed in blue ink on the record form in the "Point to ..." column.

the "Point to ..." column. After the administration of the first few items, it is not necessary to precede each item with the full verbal cue. If the examinee understands the task, the prompt may be shortened to just the word or phrase for that item printed in the record form. Because the nature of the task is self explanatory, there are no teaching items on the Verbal Knowledge subtest. If the examinee does not respond to the initial prompt, encourage the examinee to respond, then repeat the prompt. The examiner does not provide the correct answer to any items. Rapid Reference 2.3 reviews the start, reverse, discontinue, and timing rules.

The Verbal Knowledge subtest has a basal of three correct responses and a ceiling of four incorrect responses. If any of the first three items at a start point are failed, the examiner should drop back to the next earlier start point. Repeat the process of dropping back one start point until the examinee either passes the first three items in a start point, or drops back to Item 1. The examinee receives credit for any items preceding the basal items. When an examinee fails four consecutive items on a subtest, discontinue testing. For the Verbal Knowledge subtest, the examiner re-

## ≡ Rapid Reference 2.3

### Summary of Verbal Knowledge Rules

**Starting Points**

Ages 4–5: Item 1
Ages 6–7: Item 5
Age 8: Item 10
Ages 9–10: Item 15
Ages 11–15: Item 20
Ages 16–90: Item 25

**Reverse Criterion**

For ages 6 and up: Score of 0 on any of the first three items, drop back to the next earlier start point. Repeat the process of dropping back one start point until the examinee either passes all of the first three items at a start point, or drops back to Item 1.

**Discontinue Criterion**

Discontinue testing when examinee fails four consecutive items.

**Timing**

Not timed.

## ≡ Rapid Reference 2.4

### Behaviors to Note on Verbal Knowledge

- Observe the examinee's speed and response style. Does he or she analyze each picture carefully before providing a response or answer impulsively? If the examinee is impulsive, does he or she quickly change answers?
- Problems with vision may be noted on this task. Take note of whether the examinee squints his or her eyes or picks up the stimulus booklet to hold it close to his or her face.
- Note whether the examinee frequently asks to have items repeated. If he or she is not able to hold onto verbal information temporarily, this may be indicative of attention problems.
- Does the examinee use strategies such as talking his or her way through problems in order to find a solution?
- Note how the examinee deals with frustration as items become more challenging. Does the examinee eliminate less plausible responses and then try to decide which of the remaining choices is the best response? Other examinees may give up when faced with difficult items and simply respond, "I don't know."
- If an examinee has problems making up his or her mind (i.e., it is either 2 or 3), this response style may indicate anxiety or the examinee's need for feedback. Conversely, a response such as "There is no correct answer" may indicate that the examinee is defensive.

cords the letter corresponding to the examinee's response on the record form. Each item is scored as it is administered. The examiner may repeat the question if the examinee appears to not have heard it the first time or requests to have it repeated. Circle 1 in the score column if the response is correct, and 0 if it is incorrect. Rapid Reference 2.4 notes behaviors to watch for when administering this subtest.

### Riddles

The Riddles subtest measures the examinee's ability to use reasoning, integration, and logical classification skills (Kaufman & Kaufman, 2004b).

On the Riddles subtest, the examiner says a verbal riddle and the examinee points to the picture (Items 1–8) or says the word (Items 9–48) that answers the riddle. According to the test developers (Kaufman & Kaufman, 2004b), Riddles items are composed of a set of attributes or functions of an object or concept, and the examinee is required to integrate the features. The early items contain two clues, while the remaining items contain three clues each. On the more difficult items, clues are presented in a sequence that requires the examinee to consider all three clues in order to answer correctly.

Materials needed to administer the KBIT-2 Riddles subtest include the stimulus booklet and record form. Directions and verbal prompts for Items 1 through 8 are provided in the stimulus booklet. For Items 9 through 48, directions and verbal prompts are indicated on the record form. The Riddles subtest includes four teaching items on which the examiner should explain the correct answer following an error. The first two picture items (Items 1 and 2) and the first two items requiring oral responses (Items 9 and 10) are teaching items. Teaching items are indicated on the record form with blue apples. If an examinee fails a teaching item, score 0. Next, provide the correct answer using the prompt available in the stimulus book (Items 1 and 2) or on the record form (Items 9 and 10). Following the verbal prompt, repeat the item; however, score only the examinee's first response to each teaching item. If the examinee fails the second trial of the item, use your own words to restate the directions or describe the task using simple language, examples, or gestures. Teaching a task should not take more than a couple of minutes. Kaufman and Kaufman (2004b) indicated that it is acceptable to use a different language or sign language for teaching purposes. If the examinee does not understand the task after it is taught, do not continue

## DON'T FORGET

The Riddles and Matrices subtests include teaching items. If the examinee fails a teaching item, score 0 and readminister the item. If the examinee fails the second trial of a sample item, restate the directions and describe the task in your own words.

attempts at teaching the task. At this point, administer the subtest until the discontinue criterion is met.

The Riddles subtest has a basal of three correct responses and a ceiling of four incorrect responses. If any of the first three items at a start point are failed, drop back to the next earlier start point. Repeat the process of dropping back one start point until the examiner either passes the first three items in a start point, or drops back to Item 1. The examinee receives credit for any items preceding the basal items. When an examinee fails four consecutive items on a subtest, discontinue testing. Rapid Reference 2.5 reviews the start, reverse, discontinue, stop, and timing rules for the Riddles subtest.

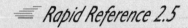

## Rapid Reference 2.5

### Summary of Riddles Rules

**Starting Points**

Ages 4–6: Item 1

Ages 7–11: Item 9

Ages 12–21: Item 14

Ages 22–65: Item 20

Ages 66–90: Item 14

**Reverse Criterion**

For ages 7 and up: Score of 0 on any of the first three items, drop back to the next earlier start point.

Repeat the process of dropping back one start point until the examinee either passes all of the first three items at a start point, or drops back to Item 1.

**Discontinue Criterion**

Discontinue testing when examinee fails four consecutive items.

**Timing**

Not timed.

There are several scoring rules that are important to note on the Riddles subtest. Examiners should study the scoring rules provided on the second page of the Riddles subtest in the stimulus booklet before administration. On all items of the Riddles subtest, the examiner may repeat items if the examinee requests it or if the examinee does not appear to hear the question. For Items 1 through 8, if the examinee points to something in the room that is a correct answer, score the item as correct. A correct oral response gets a score of 1 on Items 1 through 8; however, if the examinee provides an incorrect oral response and then points to the correct picture, score the item as correct.

For items 9 through 48, the examinee is prompted to answer riddles using a single word. If an examinee gives a multi-word response, remind him or her that the answer should be one word. Give the examinee credit if you are unsure whether a response is two words or a single compound word. For credit on items 9 through 48, the response must be a single correct word, or contain one word that is correct by itself, as long as any additional words are consistent with the riddle clues (Kaufman & Kaufman, 2004b). If the examinee gives a multi-word response and then was prompted for a one-word response, give credit if either the first or second response is correct. On the record form, parentheses are used to identify words that are not required for a correct response, but do not make the response incorrect when included. For items 9 through 48, the examiner does not need to probe ambiguous or incomplete responses. According to the *KBIT-2 Manual* (Kaufman & Kaufman, 2004b), care was taken to ensure that Riddles items are not imprecise or vague so that querying is unnecessary.

The KBIT-2 Riddles subtest may not be administered in any language other than English. Occasionally, an examinee may evaluate an individual who responds to a Riddles item in a different language. If this occurs, credit should be given for a response given in a language other than English if the examiner knows the word is consistent with a correct English response. To assist the examiner, Spanish responses to Riddles items 9 through 48 are provided in the record form.

Common correct and incorrect responses for each of the Riddles items

## ≡ Rapid Reference 2.6

### Behaviors to Note on Riddles

- Observe whether the examinee has word-finding difficulties. This might be observed in examinees that provide "I don't know" responses. Alternatively, examinees may struggle to answer questions with one-word responses.
- If the examinee responds incorrectly to a teaching item, does he or she understand the task after additional teaching?
- Be aware that many of the Riddles questions have rather lengthy verbal stimuli. Note whether inattention may be impacting the examinee's responses to such items.
- Be aware that when an examinee asks for riddles to be repeated that it may indicate poor hearing, inattention, or the need for more time to process information.
- Failure to respond within an expected amount of time (approximately 45 seconds to a minute) may be due to confusion, anxiety, slow processing, or obsessiveness.
- Take note when younger children are able to answer multiple-choice picture items 1–8 correctly but struggle to formulate verbal answers on items 9 and higher. This may indicate that the examinee is able to use deductive reasoning to recognize correct responses but has difficulties with verbal reasoning when required to formulate responses on his or her own.

9 through 48 are provided in the record form in both English and Spanish. Give credit for a response that is comparable to a listed correct response. For Riddles, record verbatim or circle the examinee's response on the record form. Score 1 in the score column if the response is correct, and 0 if the score is incorrect. Rapid Reference 2.6 reviews behaviors to watch for and note while administering this subtest.

### Matrices

The Matrices subtest was designed to assess fluid-reasoning and visual-processing abilities (Kaufman & Kaufman, 2004b). On the Matrices subtest, examinees are required to analyze the relationship or rule in a set of pictures or patterns and point to a correct response that best fits the relationship or pattern. The KBIT-2 Matrices subtest is composed of three sections of increasing difficulty. In the first section, each item depicts a single drawing at the top of the page, with a row of five drawings across the bottom of the page. The examinee chooses the item in the bottom row that is conceptually similar to the object shown above. Items in the second section are composed of analogies. Items consist of two side-by-side pairs of objects or abstract designs, with the right half of the second pair missing. The examinee identifies the drawing that completes the analogy. The third section consists of items showing a square array of drawings where a pattern or relationship is evident. The examinee identifies the drawing that maintains the pattern if inserted in the missing section of the matrix. On a few of the more difficult items, the examinee must visualize an abstract figure when part of it is folded or unfolded. The stimulus booklet and record form are needed to administer the Matrices subtest of the KBIT-2. Directions and verbal prompts for all items are provided in the stimulus booklet. After the examinee understands the task, the examiner may stop using the verbal cue "Which one goes here?"

While the Verbal Knowledge and Riddles subtests may only be administered in English, the Matrices subtest directions may be provided in any language or alternative communication style (i.e., sign language) as long as the examiner and examinee both know the language. This is possible because the examinee provides a simple verbal (i.e., says the letter) or nonverbal response (i.e., pointing). To assist Spanish-speaking examiners, each Matrices stimulus book page presents administration instructions in Spanish.

The Matrices subtest contains three unscored sample items (A, B, and C) that introduce new de-

## DON'T FORGET

While the Verbal Knowledge and Riddles subtests may only be administered in English, the Matrices subtests directions may be provided in any language as long as the examiner and examinee both know the language.

viations of the task. Teaching is allowed on the sample items and on items 1, 2, 10, 11, 23, and 24. Teaching items are indicated on the record form with blue apples. If an examinee fails a teaching item, score 0. Provide the correct answer using the prompt available in the stimulus book. Following the verbal prompt, repeat the item. If the examinee fails the second trial of the sample item, restate the directions and describe the task in your own words. If the examinee does not understand the task after teaching, discontinue attempts to teach the task. Administer the subtest until the discontinue criterion is met. Rapid Reference 2.7 reviews the start, reverse, discontinue, and timing rules for the Matrices subtest.

Consistent with basal and ceiling rules for the Verbal Knowledge and Riddles subtests, Matrices has a basal of three correct responses and a ceil-

### *Rapid Reference 2.7*

## Summary of Matrices Rules

### Starting Points
Ages 4–7: Sample A and then Item 1
Ages 8–10: Sample B and then Item 10
Ages 11–75: Sample B and then Item 15
Ages 76–90: Sample B and then Item 10

### Reverse Criterion
For ages 8 and up: Score of 0 on any of the first three items (not including the sample item), drop back to the next earlier start point. Repeat the process of dropping back one start point until the examinee either passes all of the first three items at a start point, or drops back to Sample A.

### Discontinue Criterion
Discontinue testing when examinee fails four consecutive items.

### Timing
Not timed.

ing of four incorrect responses. Sample items are not scored and are not considered in determining basal or ceiling criteria. If the examinee fails any of the first three items at a start point, drop back to the next earlier start point. Continue dropping back one start point until the examinee either passes all of the first three items in a start point, or drops back to Sample A. The examinee receives credit for any items preceding the basal items. When an examinee fails four consecutive items, discontinue testing. Rapid Reference 2.8 reviews behaviors to watch for and note when administering this subtest.

---

### ≡ Rapid Reference 2.8

#### Behaviors to Note on Matrices

- While this task is not timed, it is important to note how long it takes the examinee to process nonverbal information. Does he or she exhibit an impulsive response style or take an extended amount of time to respond?

- Watch to see how the examinee responds as task demands change somewhat on sample items B and C. If the examinee responds incorrectly to the sample item or subsequent teaching items, does he or she understand the task after additional teaching? Individuals who learn from examples may be more flexible in their thinking, while those who have more difficulty may be more concrete.

- Note whether the examinee comes up with a possible solution and then looks for that solution among the response choices. If the examinee does not use this approach, does he or she examine each of the possible solutions one by one?

- Does the examinee use strategies such as talking his or her way through problems in order to find a solution?

- Observe how the examinee responds to items as designs become increasingly complex. Does the examinee persist on difficult items or quickly give up?

- Note signs of anxiety or frustration.

## SCORING THE KBIT-2

Administration of the KBIT-2 results in several types of scores including raw scores, standard scores, confidence intervals, percentile ranks, descriptive categories, and age equivalents. The first score the examiner computes is the raw score, which is the total number of points earned on each subtest. The Verbal Knowledge and Riddles subtest raw scores are added together to provide the Verbal sum of raw scores. The Matrices raw score serves as the Nonverbal raw score. Each raw score is then converted into a Standard Score, or IQ, that has a mean of 100 and standard deviation of 15. The Standard Scores are summed and converted into an IQ Composite Standard Score. The range of IQs across the Verbal, Nonverbal, and IQ Composite scores was consistently 40 to 160 for individuals aged 7 years 4 months and older. For children 4 years 0 months to 7 years 3 months, the lower IQ limits vary somewhat for the Verbal IQ (40–57) and Nonverbal IQ (42–55), while the upper IQ limit is consistently 160.

### Converting Raw Scores

Converting the raw scores obtained on the KBIT-2 to standard scores, confidence intervals, percentile ranks, descriptive categories, and age equivalents is fairly simple. The examiner will need the following information: (a) the individual's chronological age, (b) the examinee's raw scores on the three subtests, and (c) Tables B.1, B.2. B.4, and B.5 from the *KBIT-2 Manual* (Kaufman & Kaufman, 2004b). The following list of steps outlines the process of converting raw scores to various normed scores that facilitate interpretation.

1. Using the space provided on the front left-hand corner of the KBIT-2 record form, calculate the individual's chronological age.
2. Transfer the raw scores from the inside of the record form to the front cover. The subtests are listed on the left side of the front of the record form.

3. Add the raw scores on the Verbal Knowledge and Riddles subtests to yield the Verbal raw score. Transfer the Matrices raw score to the oval labeled "Nonverbal."

4. Use Table B.1 to determine the examinee's Verbal and Nonverbal standard scores and confidence intervals. To begin, locate the page of Table B.1 that corresponds to the individual's chronological age. When locating a child or adolescent's age, disregard the days. For example, for a child who is 9 years 2 months 21 days, use the norms for 9 years 2 months. For examinees age 16 and older, disregard both the months and days. Locate the examinee's Verbal raw score in the Raw Score column of the Verbal section. Read across to the right to find the corresponding standard score, 90 percent confidence interval, and percentile rank. Record the scores on the front of the KBIT-2 record form.

5. To obtain a standard score, confidence interval, and percentile rank for the IQ Composite, add the Verbal and Nonverbal standard scores, and enter the sum on the front page of the record form in the oval labeled "Sum of Standard Scores." Using Table B.2, find the examinee's sum of standard scores and read across the row to determine the standard score for the IQ Composite, 90 percent confidence interval, and percentile rank. Record the scores on the front cover of the KBIT-2 record form. A graphical profile is provided on the bottom of the front cover of the KBIT-2 record form so that the examiner may display the individual's standard scores and 90 percent confidence intervals. To complete the graph, mark an X on the point that corresponds to the standard score. Next, mark the endpoints of the confidence interval and darken in the area to connect the endpoints.

6. To provide descriptive ranges of where the examinee's IQ Composite standard score falls relative to the normative sample, see Table B.4. Find the descriptive category that corresponds to the examinee's IQ Composite score and record it on the front cover of the record form. The descriptive categories for the KBIT-2

are based on standard deviations from the mean of 100. For example, scores within one standard deviation of the mean are in the Average descriptive category, while scores that are 2 SD below the mean are in the Below Average category. See Rapid Reference 2.9 for the range of standard scores and corresponding descriptive categories.

7. Age equivalents are optional scores that may be determined for the Verbal and Nonverbal standard score using Table B.5. Age-equivalent values are available for the range of ages (4:0 through 18:6) where growth in test performance is linear (Kaufman & Kaufman, 2004b). In order to determine the age equivalent, find the examinee's raw score for the verbal and nonverbal areas and read across to the left to locate the corresponding age equivalent.

### Special Considerations for Subtest Raw Scores of Zero

If an examinee earns a Verbal or Nonverbal raw score of zero, do not compute the corresponding Verbal or Nonverbal standard score or IQ Composite. For a Verbal raw score to be zero, this means that *both* the Verbal Knowledge and Riddles subtests scores are zero. If an individual earns a score of zero on one verbal subtest only, a Verbal standard score may still be computed. While it is highly unusual to encounter a raw score of zero when testing adults, this problem may occur when evaluating younger children. A raw score of zero indicates that the subtest did not have enough of the easier floor items to accurately evaluate the examinee's

*≡ Rapid Reference 2.9*

#### Descriptive Categories

| Range of Standard Scores | Descriptive Categories |
| --- | --- |
| 131 or greater | Upper extreme |
| 116–130 | Above average |
| 85–115 | Average |
| 70–84 | Below average |
| 69 or less | Lower extreme |

abilities. If this situation occurs, the examiner should recommend that the individual be tested on a comprehensive measure that is designed to evaluate children's skills as young as 2 or 3.

> **DON'T FORGET**
> ......................................
> If an examinee earns a Verbal or Nonverbal raw score of zero, do not compute the corresponding Verbal or Nonverbal Standard Score or IQ Composite.

## Caution in Using Descriptive Categories and Age Equivalents

According to Kaufman and Kaufman (2004b), it is not necessary to record descriptive categories for the Verbal and Nonverbal scores. In fact, unless the individual's Verbal and Nonverbal standard scores differ significantly, recording the descriptive categories is not advised. If scores fall on opposite sides of the border between descriptive categories, including the descriptive category for the Verbal and Nonverbal standard scores may give the false impression of a meaningful difference between the two domains. Kaufman and Kaufman (2004b) also advise using two categories to describe a standard score that is in one descriptive category but is within four points, or a standard error of measurement, of an adjacent descriptive category.

Kaufman and Kaufman (2004b) recommend that age equivalents be used sparingly as a supplement to standard scores and percentiles. Test authors were careful to point out that age equivalents do not rise and fall in the same manner as standard scores and percentiles. Therefore, they may appear to indicate greater or smaller differences than do standard scores or percentiles for a given raw-score difference.

## Step 1. Interpret the IQ Composite

The KBIT-2 IQ Composite is a highly reliable score (average split-half across the age span of .93;

> **DON'T FORGET**
> ......................................
> Unless an individual's Verbal and Nonverbal Standard Scores differ significantly, Kaufman and Kaufman do not advise recording descriptive categories.

## ≡ Rapid Reference 2.10

### Meredith H. (18-year-old female) Kaufman Brief Intelligence Test–Second Edition (KBIT-2) Profile

| Scale | SS | 90% Confidence Interval | Percentile Rank |
|-------|-----|------------------------|-----------------|
| Verbal | 78 | 72–86 | 7 |
| Nonverbal | 93 | 85–102 | 32 |
| IQ Composite | 83 | 77–91 | 13 |

## ≡ Rapid Reference 2.11

### Step 1: Interpret the IQ Composite

| Scale | SS | 90% Confidence Interval | Percentile Rank | Descriptive Category |
|-------|-----|------------------------|-----------------|---------------------|
| Verbal | 78 | 72–86 | 7 | Below Average |
| Nonverbal | 93 | 85–102 | 32 | Average |
| IQ Composite | 83 | 77–91 | 13 | Below Average |

Note. If there is a significant difference between the Verbal and Nonverbal standard scores of the KBIT-2, the IQ Composite should not be interpreted as a meaningful representation of the individual's overall performance.

Caution should be taken in using descriptive categories for the Verbal and Nonverbal standard scores unless there is a significant difference between scores.

average test-retest across the age span of .90). When a single indicator of an individual's cognitive ability is needed, the KBIT-2 IQ Composite is the best estimate of the person's ability. Along with the IQ Composite, the confidence interval, percentile rank, and descriptive category should be reported. While the IQ Composite is often the best single estimate of a person's abilities, Kaufman and Kaufman (2004b) encourage examiners to focus on all three standard scores (Verbal, Nonverbal, and IQ Composite).

### Step 2. Determine if the KBIT-2 Verbal-Nonverbal Standard Score Discrepancy Is Statistically Significant

The second step in KBIT-2 interpretation is to compute the size of the difference between the Verbal and Nonverbal standard scores. To assist the examiner with this process, a Score Comparison section is included on the bottom of the front page of the record form. The differences between

## ≡ *Rapid Reference 2.12*

### Step 2: Are the Verbal SS Versus the Nonverbal SS Significantly Different?

| Verbal | Nonverbal | Difference | Significant (*p* <.05) | Not Significant | Is there a significant difference? |
|--------|-----------|------------|-----------------------|-----------------|-----------------------------------|
| 78 | 93 | 15 | 13 | <13 | Yes |

### Step 2 Decision Box

| | |
|---|---|
| If the answer is no, there is not a significant difference between the Verbal and Nonverbal standard scores. | → Explain the meaning of the standard scores not being significantly different. No further interpretation of the KBIT-2 is necessary. Do not proceed to Step 3. |
| If the answer is yes, there is a significant difference between the Verbal and Nonverbal standard scores. | → Continue on to Step 3. |

Note. Meredith H. is an 18-year-old adult. Difference levels required for statistical difference for children ages 4–10 and adults ages 56–90 vary.

the KBIT-2 Verbal and Nonverbal standard scores required for statistical significance are provided in Table B.6 of the *KBIT-2 Manual*. The critical values are provided for the <.05 and <.01 levels of significance across four age groups (ages 4, 5–10, 11–55, and 56–90). If the individual's standard score difference is equal to or greater than the value shown on the *p* <.01 column, circle <.01 in the Significance of Difference Section on the record form. If the difference is in the range of values shown in the *p* <.05, circle <.05. If the difference is less than the values shown in the *p* <.05 column, circle NS, for "nonsignificant."

If a significant Verbal versus Nonverbal standard score discrepancy is not found, then assume that the individual's overall verbal and nonverbal skills are evenly developed and additional steps of KBIT-2 interpretation are unnecessary. If the difference score is equal to or larger than the .05 critical value, it is statistically significant. If there is a significant difference between the Verbal standard score and Nonverbal standard score in either direction (Verbal SS > Nonverbal SS or Nonverbal SS > Verbal SS), the IQ Composite becomes less meaningful and should not be interpreted as the best indicator of an examinee's abilities. If a significant difference is found, move to Step 3 to determine whether the difference between the Verbal and Nonverbal standard scores is *meaningful*.

**Step 3. Are the Verbal and Nonverbal Standard Score Differences Unusually Large?**

In order for a discrepancy between the Verbal and Nonverbal standard scores to be *meaningful*, the difference must be rare or occur in a relatively small percentage of individuals. In this next step we determine how frequently the difference between standard scores occurs in the general population. Table B.7 in the *KBIT-2 Manual* (Kaufman & Kaufman, 2004b) provides five different degrees of infrequency: 16 percent, 10 percent, 5 percent, 2 percent, and 1 percent. Using the individual's age, locate the value or range that includes the individual's standard score discrepancy and circle the percentage frequency on the front cover of the record form

≡ *Rapid Reference 2.13*

### Step 3: Is the Verbal Versus Nonverbal SS Difference Unusually Large?

| Verbal vs. Nonverbal SS Difference | Size of Difference Needed of Abnormality | Does size meet unusually large criteria? |
|:---:|:---:|:---:|
| 15 | 24 | No |

### Step 3 Decision Box

| | | |
|---|---|---|
| If an *unusually* large difference is found | → then this *unusual* discrepancy should be interpreted. | → Explain the *unusually* large Verbal and Nonverbal difference. |
| If *no unusually* large difference is found | → then you must determine if noted difference is interpretable. | → Explain the noted difference. |

under the heading "Frequency of Occurrence of Difference in the Score Comparison" section. Sixteen percent represents the most liberal level of discrepancy, while more conservative criteria are represented by 10 percent, 5 percent, 2 percent, and 1 percent. Kaufman and Kaufman (2004b) advocate the use of 10 percent for determining unusually large differences between test scores. If an individual's discrepancy is smaller than the value shown for his or her age group in Table B.7 at the 16 percent (1 standard deviation), the difference should not be considered infrequent or unusual, even if it is statistically significant.

**DON'T FORGET**

Examiners are cautioned against interpreting implications of a *meaningful* Verbal and Nonverbal KBIT-2 difference and should recommend comprehensive testing.

Examiners are cautioned against interpreting implications of a *meaningful* Verbal and Nonverbal KBIT-2 difference, and should recommend comprehensive testing.

## Determining Scaled Scores for the Verbal Knowledge and Riddles Subtests

Kaufman and Kaufman (2004b) did not design the two KBIT-2 verbal subtests, Verbal Knowledge and Riddles, to measure distinct verbal abilities. However, there may be circumstances in which it is useful to compare performance on the two measures, or situations may arise when one or the other subtests cannot be administered. For these purposes, Table B.8 in the *KBIT-2 Manual* (Kaufman and Kaufman, 2004b) provides norms for these two subtests using scaled scores (mean of 10, standard deviation of 3). While a scaled score on one subtest cannot be used for obtaining a Verbal score or IQ Composite standard score, the purpose of scaled scores is to provide useful normative information about an individual's abilities. When comparing Verbal Knowledge and Riddles scaled scores, a difference of three points or greater is significant at the .05 level.

## STRENGTHS AND WEAKNESSES OF THE TEST

In the next section, we highlight major strengths and weaknesses of the KBIT-2 in the areas of test development, administration and scoring, reliability and validity, standardization, and interpretation. Information is provided using the Rapid Reference format to provide information in a user-friendly format. (See Rapid Reference 2.14.)

## CLINICAL APPLICATIONS OF THE TEST

In order to provide evidence of the clinical sensitivity of the KBIT-2, data were collected with various special populations including individuals with learning disabilities, speech/language disability, Attention-Deficit/

## ≡ Rapid Reference 2.14

### Strengths and Weaknesses of KBIT-2

#### Strengths

- KBIT-2 can be used across a wide range of ages 4–90.

- Normative IQs range from 40–160 for most ages and provide a high ceiling for children and low floor for adolescents and adults.

- Test authors provide theoretical explanation for using lower start points for individuals ages 76–90 on the Matrices subtest.

- KBIT-2 is normed such that if the examinee fails the second trial of a teaching item on Riddles and Matrices subtests, examiner may use own words to restate directions or describe the task more generally using additional examples. It is also permissible to use a different language for teaching.

- Care was taken to drop potentially offensive or biased items from Verbal Knowledge subtest.

- Subtests have many common rules that facilitate easy administration. For example, basal and ceiling rules are consistent across subtests. Similarly, all items are worth 0 or 1 point.

#### Weaknesses

- Because a one-word response is required for Riddles subtests, limited information is obtained regarding an examinee's expressive vocabulary abilities.

- Split-half reliability is not excellent for the Nonverbal score when assessing young children ages 4 and 5 (mean = .78).

- KBIT-2 IQ Composite correlates .76 and .77 with the WISC-III and WISC-IV Full Scale IQs.

- KBIT-2 Nonverbal score correlations with WISC-III PIQ (.53), WISC-IV PRI (.56), and WAIS-III (.79) are low.

- While verbal subtests assess general information, receptive vocabulary, and verbal reasoning, the ability to measure expressive vocabulary is limited.

- The KBIT-2 samples only limited areas of cognitive functioning and does not measure processing speed or working memory constructs.

(continued)

- Matrices subtest may be administered in languages other than English as long as the language is shared by examiner and examinee.
- While Riddles subtest is not to be administered in languages other than English, responses provided by examinee in other languages may be scored as correct if the examiner knows the language and the answer is equivalent to a correct English response. To facilitate score, correct Spanish responses are provided in record form for Riddles Items 9–48.
- Artwork is colorful and appealing.
- Split-half reliability coefficients are excellent for the IQ Composite and Verbal standard score with means of .93 and .90, respectively.
- Test-retest reliabilities are favorable for the IQ Composite, Verbal standard score, and Nonverbal standard score with means of .90, .91, and .83, respectively.
- The KBIT-2 was well stratified and closely matches U.S. population based on March 2001 Current Population Survey.

- KBIT-2 Matrices subtest is not appropriate for individuals with significant visual deficits.

- Sample collection procedures and quality control measures were taken to ensure data integrity.

- Tables are provided in the *KBIT-2 Manual* to indicate Verbal SS and Nonverbal SS differences required for significance. Frequencies of Verbal SS and Nonverbal SS differences based on ability are also provided.

- Authors provide useful explanations on appropriateness of providing descriptive ranges and age-equivalent scores.

- Although less reliable than interpreting the Verbal SS, examiners may compare Verbal Knowledge and Riddles subtest scaled scores.

Hyperactivity Disorder, Mental Retardation, gifted and talented, traumatic brain injury, and dementia. Study results are reported in the *KBIT-2 Manual* (Kaufman & Kaufman, 2004b, pp. 164–65). Across studies, sample sizes were small, ranging from 12 to 95 participants. Individuals with Mental Retardation exhibited very low means (Verbal SS = 63.1, Nonverbal SS = 65.3, IQ Composite SS = 61.1) on the KBIT-2, indicating that this measure demonstrates the ability to effectively assess individuals with lower cognitive abilities. The mean scores for children and adolescents in gifted programs ranged from 110 to 115 while individuals with ADHD or a learning disability had means near 90 on all three KBIT-2 scores. Examinees with speech/language disability exhibited slightly lower Verbal (M = 85) than Nonverbal scores (M = 88). The traumatic brain injury and dementia groups had mean standard scores of approximately 75 across all three KBIT-2 indices.

### 🐿 TEST YOURSELF 🐿

1. **Test developers hoped to accomplish which of the following when revising the original K-BIT?**

   (a) update norms

   (b) develop alternative subtests to measure verbal ability

   (c) develop alternative subtests to measure nonverbal ability

   (d) both a and b

2. **According to growth curve studies conducted by Kaufman and Kaufman (2004a),**

   (a) crystallized abilities decline at a later age than fluid abilities

   (b) fluid abilities decline at a later age than crystallized abilities

   (c) crystallized and fluid abilities decline at roughly the same age

   (d) there is no consistent pattern of decline with age

3. **The Verbal Knowledge and Riddles subtests may be administered in Spanish?** True or false?

4. **Basal and ceiling rules are consistent across KBIT-2 subtests.** True or false?

5. **If an examinee fails a teaching item on the Riddles or Matrices subtests, the examiner should**

   (a) discontinue testing

   (b) provide a second trial and give credit if the response is correct

   (c) provide a second trial but do not give credit if the response is correct

   (d) immediately provide direction in your own words

6. **Mike, age 5, is administered the KBIT-2 and earns a raw score of zero on the Riddles subtest. You should**

   (a) calculate the IQ Composite only

   (b) calculate neither the Verbal SS or the IQ Composite

   (c) calculate the Verbal SS, Nonverbal SS, and the IQ Composite

   (d) consider the entire test invalid

7. **For individuals age 7 years 4 months to 90 years, the Verbal, Nonverbal, and IQ Composite scores range from 60 to 130.** True or false?

8. **According to Kaufman and Kaufman (2004b), providing descriptive categories**

   (a) is not recommended in most cases

   (b) may give the false impression of a meaningful Verbal SS and Nonverbal SS difference

   (c) is useful when examinee's Verbal and Nonverbal SS differ significantly

   (d) all of the above

9. **When determining whether Verbal and Nonverbal Standard Score differences are unusually large, Kaufman and Kaufman (2004b) advocate using which of the following cut-off percentages?**

   (a) 16%

   (b) 10%

   (c) 5%

   (d) 1%

10. **When might it be useful to determine the scaled score for the Verbal Knowledge and/or Riddles subtests?**

   (a) when either of the subtests cannot be administered

   (b) to compare distinct receptive and expressive vocabulary abilities

   (c) to assess for a language-based learning disability

   (d) none of the above

*Answers:* 1. d; 2. a; 3. False; 4. True; 5. c; 6. b; 7. False; 8. d; 9. b; 10. a

Three

# THE REYNOLDS INTELLECTUAL SCREENING TEST (RIST)

The RIST (Reynolds & Kamphaus, 2003a) is a two-subtest, extremely rapidly administered and scored brief intelligence test requiring 8 to 12 minutes for administration. It is standardized on 2,438 individuals from ages 3 years through 94 years. Hand-scoring requires only several minutes; however, a computer-scoring program is available (it is included in the RIAS-SP, which also scores the Reynolds Intellectual Assessment Scales; see www.parinc.com) that also provides interpretive suggestions and generates a report that can be given to examinees over age 18 years or to parents of younger examinees. The two RIST subtests, entitled "Guess What" (GWH) and "Odd Item Out" (OIO), are taken from the Reynolds Intellectual Assessment Scales (RIAS; Reynolds & Kamphaus, 2003b). These subtests are described in Table 3.1 and sample the domains of verbal or crystallized intelligence and nonverbal or fluid intelligence. Ordinarily, we would not have included a derivative work in this volume for reasons given in Chapter 1 of this book and for reasons explicated in Kaufman and Lichtenberger (2006). However, these criticisms of derivative tests (brief tests derived from a comprehensive parent scale) do not apply to the RIST. The RIST subtests are administered in exactly the same order as on the parent scale, have the same items, and

Portions of this chapter are adapted with permission of the copyrightholder, Psychological Assessment Resources, Inc., from C. R. Reynolds & R. W. Kamphaus (2003), *Reynolds Intellectual Assessment Scales and Reynolds Intellectual Screening Test: Professional Manual,* Chapter 7, Lutz, FL: PAR, Inc.

## Table 3.1 Subtest Names and Descriptions for the RIST

**Verbal Component**

Guess What (GWH)      On this task, examinees are given a set of 2–4 oral clues about an object or a concept and asked to deduce what is being described. This task assesses verbal reasoning, or crystallized intelligence, in combination with vocabulary, language development, and general knowledge.

**Nonverbal Component**

Odd-Item Out (OIO)      On this task, examinees are presented with a card with 5 to 7 pictures on it. The examinee must then determine which picture does not belong with the others. This reverse-analogy task measures nonverbal reasoning and fluid intelligence in combination with spatial ability, visual imaging skills, and analogical reasoning.

follow the identical testing procedures. Extensive reliability and validity data are provided as well.

As Reynolds and Kamphaus (2003a) note, the RIST is intended as a brief measure of intelligence that is particularly useful in the screening of intellectual level when individual test administration is desirable and in other applications as described in Chapter 1 of this volume. The subtests include one from the domain of verbal reasoning (GWH) and one from nonverbal reasoning (OIO), each scaled to a $T$-score (mean = 50, SD = 10). A RIST intelligence index is provided as a summary score set to the traditional IQ metric of a

> **CAUTION**
>
> The RIST has a very wide age range, being normed from 3 years through 94 years. Being skilled at administration and scoring of the RIST, while necessary to a successful evaluation, is also insufficient. Be sure you are familiar with and have experience handling the special challenges that can be posed by preschool children, teenagers, and senior adults in the context of intellectual assessment.

## ≋ *Rapid Reference 3.1*

### The Reynolds Intellectual Screening Test (RIST)

**Authors:** Cecil R. Reynolds & Randy W. Kamphaus

**Publication Date:** 2003

**What the test measures:** Verbal, nonverbal, and overall intelligence

**Administration time:** 8–12 minutes

**Qualifications of examiner:** Supervised experience in individual test administration and scoring (also see text).

**Publisher:** Psychological Assessment Resources, Inc. (PAR)
16204 N. Florida Avenue
Lutz, FL 33549
800-331-TEST (8378)
www.parinc.com

**Prices** (as of August 1, 2006): Starter set (Manual, stimulus book, 25 record forms), $195.00
RIAS-SP CD-ROM Computer Scoring Program, unlimited use, $165.00

$M = 100$ and $SD = 15$. Additional score types are provided including percentile ranks, normal curve equivalents, $z$-scores, and stanines. (See Rapid References 3.1–3.3.)

According to conventional wisdom regarding screening for clinical disorders, it is preferable to expend extra assessment resources to evaluate clients with even a minimal risk of having a disorder (i.e., increasing the rate of false positives) than to fail to evaluate individuals in need of treatment (i.e., increasing the rate of false negatives). This rubric underlies the administration, scoring, interpretation, and psychometric properties of the RIST (Reynolds & Kamphaus, 2003a).

## DON'T FORGET

The RIST intelligence index ranges over 8 SDs, providing scores from 40 to 160 at most ages.

## ≡ *Rapid Reference 3.2*

### The RIAS-SP Computer Scoring Program for the RIST

- Provides unlimited scoring and report generation for both the RIST and the RIAS, based on subtest raw scores entered by the user.
- The RIST Score Report includes the individual's demographic information, a score summary, the RIST Profile, and narrative text.
- Generates profile graphs with the ability to overlay profiles from a client's prior test administrations (if any).
- Produces three different score reports and two client feedback reports.
- Includes built-in, easy-to-use report editing features including cut and drop.
- Gives users the ability to select specific report components for inclusion in the printed report.
- Includes an optional user-defined password feature to ensure confidentiality and security of client data.
- Exports client data for use in various spreadsheet and database programs; exports score and feedback reports to common word processing programs.
- Network version is available.

**Hardware Requirements:** Windows* 95/NT 4.0 with Internet Explorer 4.0 or higher;
Windows* 98/Me/2000/XP;
CD-ROM drive for installation;
Internet connection or telephone for software activation

## USER QUALIFICATIONS

The user qualifications for the RIST are not as stringent as those for its parent scale—the RIAS—when used solely for screening. The training required for administration and scoring when used as a screening tool is more lenient because the interpretation made by the individual conducting the screening is far simpler—to refer or not to refer. Prekindergarten

### ≡ Rapid Reference 3.3

**The RIST Provides Several Different Score Metrics for the Convenience of the Examiner**

- Percentile Ranks
- Traditional IQ-scaling — M = 100 — SD = 15
- T-scores — M = 50 — SD = 10
- z-scores — M = 0 — SD = 1
- Normal Curve Equivalents (NCEs) — M = 50 — SD = 21.06
- Stanines — M = 5 — SD = 2

**DON'T FORGET**

User qualifications for the RIST vary depending upon the applications being made. When used purely for screening purposes, less formal training and knowledge of psychometrics is required compared to circumstances wherein more critical clinical decisions are at issue.

screening is an excellent example of a ubiquitous screening process in which the individual conducting the intelligence/cognitive development screening seldom has, but may have, advanced training in psychological measurement. Depending on the school district, this screening is conducted by teachers, educational diagnosticians, lead teachers, classroom aides, speech pathologists, social workers, school psychologists, and parent volunteers, among others. The RIST may also be used for screening by this diverse array of clinicians (Reynolds & Kamphaus, 2003a). It is crucial that RIST users, regardless of their background or the purposes of testing, always be trained to do the following, at a minimum:

- adhere to standardized administration and scoring procedures
- check scoring accuracy and obtain a criterion level of errorless protocols as part of the training process

- consult the screening process supervisor when there are any concerns about a person's results

Regardless of the screening use, continuing quality control of administration, scoring, and decision-making processes will be necessary when the RIST is used for assessment of intelligence of psychiatric patients, children and adolescents referred for emotional and behavioral disorders, vocational evaluations, and in other circumstances in which decision-making goes beyond the refer/do not refer threshold issue. Comprehensive knowledge of theories of intelligence, cognitive science, developmental psychology, and psychometrics and measurement theory, coupled with formal supervised experience with comprehensive measures of intelligence, and so forth, are required for individuals who supervise and train examiners who use the RIST for screening purposes.

## STANDARDIZATION AND PSYCHOMETRIC PROPERTIES

The RIST manual provides great detail regarding the standardization of the test. Extensive information on item development and subsequent psychometric properties of the RIST are given therein as well. This information is summarized in the following sections.

### Item Development

Items for the RIST were written by the authors initially to represent the constructs to be assessed as described for each subtest in Table 3.1. Items were subsequently reviewed by multiple doctoral-level psychologists from several specialties (clinical psychology, clinical neuropsychology, school psychology, and measurement and statistics) for coherence with the constructs to be assessed, objectivity and interscorer agreement, ambiguities in the language or pictures used, potential cultural biases, and for adherence to good item-writing principles. Approximately five times as many items were generated as desired for the final form to ensure a sufficient item pool for strong reliability values across the entire age range of 3 years to 94 years. Based upon this review, items were modified for clarity, scoring, and other factors, while some items were eliminated.

Next, a diverse panel of psychologists representing multiple ethnic and religious minority groups of both genders reviewed all items for cultural clarity, offensiveness, or other objectionable content. About 10 percent of the item pool was eliminated or underwent significant modifications based on these reviews. A large-scale empirical tryout followed that ultimately winnowed the item pool to the standardization version. Once the standardization data were collected, items were again analyzed using multiple statistical procedures in an iterative fashion to ensure items achieved the following goals:

1. Items demonstrating significant levels of differential item functioning (DIF) by gender or ethnicity were disallowed;
2. subtest internal consistency reliability estimates of .90 or higher for both subtests across age and for the total sample;
3. items that could be easily, clearly ordered by ascending order of difficulty;
4. sufficient easy and hard items to avoid significant floor and ceiling effects; and,
5. a steep item difficulty gradient to allow for a brief administration time.

Extensive DIF analyses were conducted to detect items biased by gender or ethnicity on an iterative basis following each round of item analysis (the latter using a true score model). These analyses are described in detail in Reynolds and Kamphaus (2003a), pages 61 through 63.

## Standardization

The RIST was normed on a sample of 2,438 individuals from 41 of the 50 United States. Data collection occurred between 1999 and 2002. Sampling was designed to match the U.S. population on the characteristics of age, gender, ethnicity, educational attainment (for ages 3–18, parent educational level was employed), and region of residence as defined by the U.S. Bureau of the Census, 2001 Current Population Survey. The obtained sample was a close match to the population statistics with only minor deviations present. To correct these minor deviations, a poststratification weighting procedure was employed to create a near-perfect match to the Census statistics.

## Scaling

The various RIST standardized scores were devised from raw scores of the weighted standardization sample using the continuous norming procedure first espoused by Gorsuch (1983) and later modified by Zachary and Gorsuch (1985). Continuous norming uses methods of linear and nonlinear curve fitting across all ages in a normative sample, fitting four moments of the score distribution: mean, standard deviation, skewness, and kurtosis. Percentiles are then determined based on the best fit of the data to the curves determined by use of the entire sample at every normative level, thus maximizing the accuracy of the derived scores. The percentiles are then used to derive the various scaled score metrics provided. A detailed description of this process is given in Reynolds and Kamphaus (2003a).

## Reliability of RIST Scores

Internal consistency reliability estimates for the RIST subtests are quite high. As can be seen in Table 3.2 (based on the standardization sample data), most of the coefficients are above .90 across age, gender, and ethnicity. Stability

**DON'T FORGET**

The RIST standardized scores were derived using the continuous norming procedure, which maximizes the accuracy of derived scores.

**DON'T FORGET**

The median internal consistency reliability coefficients for the RIST subtests' and composite scores across age is .90 or higher.

**Table 3.2 Reliability Coefficients of the RIST Subtest Scores by Gender, Ethnicity, and Age Groups**

| | Subtest | | | | | | | | | |
|---|---|---|---|---|---|---|---|---|---|---|
| | GWH | | | | OIO | | | | GWH | OIO |
| Age (years) | W | AA | M | F | W | AA | M | F | Total Sample | Total Sample |
| 3 | .89 | .83 | .92 | .86 | .94 | .92 | .93 | .93 | .89 | .93 |
| 4 | .93 | .91 | .90 | .94 | .91 | .92 | .92 | .92 | .92 | .91 |
| 5 | .95 | .92 | .95 | .95 | .91 | .89 | .91 | .90 | .95 | .90 |
| 6 | .93 | .95 | .92 | .95 | .95 | .94 | .92 | .96 | .93 | .94 |
| 7 | .92 | .96 | .94 | .92 | .95 | .94 | .95 | .95 | .93 | .95 |
| 8 | .91 | .90 | .94 | .91 | .94 | .95 | .93 | .95 | .92 | .94 |
| 9 | .91 | .92 | .93 | .92 | .95 | .88 | .95 | .95 | .92 | .95 |
| 10 | .90 | .92 | .90 | .91 | .94 | .92 | .92 | .95 | .91 | .94 |
| 11–12 | .87 | .91 | .90 | .89 | .94 | .95 | .95 | .94 | .89 | .94 |
| 13–14 | .88 | .91 | .91 | .90 | .94 | .94 | .93 | .95 | .90 | .94 |
| 15–16 | .88 | .94 | .93 | .91 | .95 | .96 | .95 | .95 | .91 | .95 |
| 17–19 | .87 | .89 | .90 | .94 | .93 | .90 | .94 | .94 | .92 | .94 |
| 20–34 | .92 | .93 | .93 | .91 | .94 | .95 | .95 | .93 | .92 | .95 |
| 35–54 | .94 | .96 | .94 | .95 | .95 | .95 | .95 | .95 | .95 | .95 |
| 55–74 | .91 | .94 | .92 | .92 | .94 | .97 | .95 | .95 | .79 | .95 |
| 75–94 | .93 | .98 | .94 | .93 | .95 | .80 | .96 | .95 | .94 | .95 |

*Note*: GWH = Guess What; VRZ = Verbal Reasoning; OIO = Odd-Item Out; W = White; AA = African American; M = Male; F = Female.

coefficients are likewise strong at .89 over a 3-week interval for GWH and .77 for OIO for the full age range. Little variability is seen in these values across age.

The internal consistency and test-retest reliability coefficients for the RIST composite appear to be more than sufficient for virtually all purposes for which brief IQ tests may be deemed appropriate. The RIST composite yielded a median standard error of measurement of 3.35 and a median internal consistency coefficient of .95 (see Table 3.3). Furthermore, uncorrected $(r_u)$ and corrected $(C\text{-}r_u)$ stability coefficients of .80 and .84, respectively, were obtained for the RIST composite. These data suggest that the reliability for the RIST composite is adequate for it to serve

**Table 3.3  Standard Errors of Measurement and Reliability Coefficients of the RIST Composite Index by Age, Gender, and Ethnicity**

| Age (years) | $SE_M$ | Reliability Coefficients | | | | |
| | | Total Sample | Male | Female | White | African American |
|---|---|---|---|---|---|---|
| 3 | 3.67 | .94 | .95 | .93 | .94 | .90 |
| 4 | 3.35 | .95 | .94 | .96 | .96 | .94 |
| 5 | 3.00 | .96 | .97 | .96 | .97 | .94 |
| 6 | 3.00 | .96 | .95 | .97 | .96 | .96 |
| 7 | 3.35 | .95 | .96 | .96 | .96 | .97 |
| 8 | 3.00 | .96 | .96 | .95 | .95 | .96 |
| 9 | 3.00 | .96 | .95 | .96 | .95 | .93 |
| 10 | 3.67 | .94 | .93 | .95 | .96 | .88 |
| 11–12 | 3.35 | .95 | .95 | .94 | .94 | .95 |
| 13–14 | 3.67 | .94 | .94 | .94 | .93 | .95 |
| 15–16 | 3.35 | .95 | .96 | .95 | .94 | .97 |
| 17–19 | 3.35 | .95 | .94 | .97 | .92 | .92 |
| 20–34 | 3.00 | .96 | .97 | .95 | .96 | .97 |
| 35–54 | 2.60 | .97 | .97 | .97 | .97 | .97 |
| 55–74 | 3.35 | .95 | .95 | .96 | .95 | .98 |
| 75–94 | 2.60 | .97 | .98 | .96 | .96 | .86 |
| **Median** | **3.35** | **.95** | | | | |

*Source.* From Reynolds & Kamphaus (2003a, p. 121) with permission of PAR, Inc.

*Note. N* = 2,438.

as either a first or second screening gate and that it may be used for other brief intelligence testing purposes described throughout this volume. In fact, the internal consistency reliability and stability of RIST scores are comparable to those of intelligence tests of far greater length.

## Validity of RIST Score Interpretation

Two types of construct validity evidence are available for the recommended RIST score interpretations (in addition to information on the item development process): criterion-related and differential validity. Criterion-related validity was assessed in three investigations via correlations with the WISC-III, the WAIS-III, and the WIAT (see Table 3.4).

**Table 3.4  Correlations Between the RIST Composite Index and Other Measures of Intelligence and Achievement**

|  | | RIST | |
| --- | --- | --- | --- |
| Measure | Correlations | M | SD |
| WISC-III[a] |  | 102.80 | 15.96 |
| VIQ | .86 |  |  |
| PIQ | .47 |  |  |
| FSIQ | .83 |  |  |
| WAIS-III[b] |  | 96.29 | 24.40 |
| VIQ | .63 |  |  |
| PIQ | .66 |  |  |
| FSIQ | .67 |  |  |
| WIAT[c] |  | 102.46 | 13.88 |
| Reading | .61 |  |  |
| Math | .69 |  |  |
| Language | .67 |  |  |
| Writing | .56 |  |  |
| Total Composite | .66 |  |  |

*Source.* Adapted from Reynolds and Kamphaus (2003a, p. 122) with permission of PAR, Inc.

[a]$N = 54$.

[b]$N = 31$.

[c]$N = 78$.

The purpose of the first two investigations of evidence based on variables external to the test was to assess whether or not the RIST correlated highly enough with well-known comprehensive measures of intelligence to be considered an intelligence screener, and yet not so high as to be considered the same as those tests. The RIST index correlated .83 with the WISC-III FSIQ and .67 with the WAIS-III FSIQ. The RIST composite index was also correlated with the RIAS Composite Intelligence Index (CIX) at four age levels and for the total standardization sample of 2,438. The RIST/RIAS CIX correlations ranged only from .91 to .94 across age and was .93 for the total sample. These results strongly suggest that the RIST is an appropriate screener for intelligence.

The purpose of the third study was to assess whether the RIST could serve as a screener for intelligence on the basis of high score correlations with meaningful outcome variables. The correlations between the RIAS and a measure of academic achievement were high. In fact, Table 3.4 shows that the RIST correlated .61 with reading, .69 with mathematics, .67 with language, .56 with writing, and .66 with the WIAT total composite. All of these correlations are highly similar to those found for more comprehensive measures of intelligence (see Kamphaus, 2001, for a review).

Discriminant validity of the RIST was assessed in several studies of clinical samples, which included individuals with diagnoses of ADHD, LD, Bipolar Disorder, traumatic brain injury, stroke/CVA, Schizophrenia, dementia, and Mental Retardation (see Table 3.5). The samples with Mental Retardation and dementia were of particular interest because these two conditions are defined, in part, by the presence of intellectual impairment. For both groups, the mean RIST composite score was in the mid-70s. These results provide evidence that the RIST can differentiate examinees with intellectual impairment from those without such impairment.

## ADMINISTERING AND SCORING THE RIST

The RIST subtests were designed for ease of administration and scoring and to reduce various confounds such as speed of performance, fine motor problems, and reading skill in the assessment of intelligence. There

## Table 3.5  RIST Composite Index Scores for Various Clinical Groups

| Clinical group | $N$ | M | SD |
|---|---|---|---|
| **Organic syndromes and related groups** | | | |
| Mental Retardation | 26 | 76.46 | 20.45 |
| Traumatic brain injury | 44 | 94.05 | 10.85 |
| Stroke/cerebrovascular accident (CVA) | 19 | 95.05 | 14.57 |
| Seizure disorder | 9 | 81.44 | 16.76 |
| Dementia | 27 | 75.48 | 19.98 |
| Deaf/hearing-deficient[a] | 14 | 102.43 | 13.74 |
| **Learning disabilities and ADHD groups** | | | |
| Child learning disabilities | 60 | 89.55 | 11.54 |
| Child ADHD | 49 | 93.82 | 14.49 |
| Adult learning disabilities | 10 | 96.90 | 14.36 |
| Adult ADHD | 11 | 87.82 | 18.80 |
| **Psychiatric groups** | | | |
| Anxiety | 23 | 84.17 | 26.51 |
| Depression | 39 | 87.08 | 22.76 |
| Schizophrenia | 33 | 89.36 | 15.45 |
| Bipolar Disorder | 9 | 93.56 | 11.87 |
| Polysubstance abuse | 134 | 93.26 | 19.27 |

*Source.* From Reynolds & Kamphaus (2003a, p. 123) with permission of PAR, Inc.

[a]Deaf/hearing-deficient scores were obtained using nonstandard administration procedures. See text in chapter 6 of Reynolds and Kamphaus (2003a) for an explanation.

are no manipulatives for the examinee, no bonus points for quick performance, and no reading or use of written words.

The instructions for each RIST subtest are very brief (i.e., not more than two sentences), and scoring is entirely objective (interscorer reliability coefficients of 1.00 are reported in the manual for both subtests). A sample item is provided for each subtest. Although OIO has a time limit for responses, research during the national tryout confirmed that it is a power test and not a speeded test. The RIST record form is a great aid to accurate, efficacious administration as well since it contains all of the necessary instructions for administration and for derivation of the subtest raw scores. Each subtest has a basal and a ceiling rule accompanied by age-designated starting points. Each is reviewed in the following.

## DON'T FORGET

The interscorer reliability coefficient for each RIST subtest is 1.00.

### Subtest I. Guess What (GWH)

Materials: Record Form, Professional Manual, bookstand, and/or clipboard

Time Limit: None

#### *Description*

The Guess What subtest measures vocabulary knowledge in combination with reasoning skills that are predicated on language development and fund of information. The questions pertain to physical objects, abstract concepts, and well-known places and historical figures from a variety of cultures and geographic locations. Many disciplines are represented among the test questions.

#### *Begin Rule*

All examinees begin the subtest with the sample item, regardless of age. The sample item may be repeated, if necessary. Regardless of the examinee's performance on the sample item, proceed to the appropriate starting-point item according to the examinee's chronological age and begin administering the test items. The age-based starting points are indicated on the Record Form.

#### *Basal Level*

A basal level consists of two consecutive correct responses to the test items. However, some very young children or others with low ability levels may not obtain a basal level. When a basal cannot be obtained, the subtest may still be given, but the derived score may overestimate the examinee's ability. If the examinee does not provide correct responses on the first two test items (i.e., excluding the sample item), the Reverse Rule is applied.

### Reverse Rule

If the examinee fails to obtain a basal level on the first two test items, administer the GWH items in reverse order, beginning with the item immediately preceding the starting-point item for that examinee. Continue administering the items in reverse order until a basal level is obtained. Once a basal level is obtained in this manner, return to the point at which you began administering the items in reverse order and continue testing with the next item unless the End Rule criterion has been met.

### Discontinue Rule

Stop administering GWH when the examinee provides 0-point responses on three consecutive items (i.e., excluding the sample item).

### General Information

The GWH questions are read in a typical, conversational manner with normal inflection. The examinee's responses are written verbatim in the space provided on the Record Form. If the examinee does not respond to the item within a few seconds, does not hear the item clearly, or requests that the item be repeated, the item may be repeated. Each item may only be repeated one time.

---

**DON'T FORGET**

On GWH, discontinue testing after three consecutive 0-point responses.

---

**DON'T FORGET**

On GWH, each item may be repeated if necessary, but only once.

---

### Scoring

GWH items are scored 1 point for each correct response and 0 for each incorrect response. The sample item is not scored. Correct responses for each item are printed on the RIST Record Form. For selected items, alternative responses that can be accepted as correct (and awarded 1 point each) are listed in Appendix D of the RIST

Manual (Reynolds & Kamphaus, 2003a). Examinees are given 1-point credit for each item below the basal level and 0 for all items beyond the last item administered. The GWH total raw score is the sum of the raw scores obtained across all items (excluding the sample item).

If an examinee self-corrects an incorrect response to a previous item, credit should be given for the new correct response. Likewise, if an examinee changes an earlier correct response to an incorrect response at any time during the test session, go back to that item on the RIST Record Form and rescore the item as 0.

## Subtest 2. Odd-Item Out (OIO)

Materials: Record Form, Professional Manual, Stimulus Book 1 (Odd-Item Out), Stop Watch (or watch with a second hand), clipboard

Time Limit: Allow a maximum of 30 seconds for the examinee to begin the first response to an item. Allow a maximum of 20 seconds for the examinee to begin the second response to an item.

### Description

The Odd-Item Out subtest measures reasoning skills. For each item, the examinee is presented with a picture card containing five to seven figures or drawings. One of the figures or drawings on the picture card has a distinguishing characteristic, making it different from the others. For each item, the examinee is given two chances to identify the figure or drawing that is different from the others. Two points are awarded for a correct response given on the first attempt. One point is awarded for a correct response given on the second attempt (i.e., if the first attempt response was incorrect).

### Begin Rule

All examinees begin the subtest with the two sample items. Once the sample items are administered, testing begins with the age-designated item as indicated on the RIST Record Form.

## Basal Level

A basal level on OIO consists of two consecutive 2-point responses (i.e., correct responses obtained on the first attempts). However, some very young children or others with low ability levels may not obtain a basal level. When a basal level cannot be obtained, the subtest may still be given, but the derived score may overestimate the examinee's ability. If the examinee does not provide 2-point responses to the first two items administered (excluding the two sample items) then apply the Reverse Rule to continue testing.

## Reverse Rule

If the examinee does not obtain 2 points on each of the first two items administered, administer the items in reverse order, beginning with the item immediately preceding the starting item for that examinee. Continue administering the items in reverse order until a basal level is obtained. Once a basal level is obtained in this manner, return to the point at which you began administering the items in reverse order and continue testing with the next item unless the Discontinue Rule criterion has been met.

## Discontinue Rule

Stop testing on OIO when the examinee provides 0-point responses (i.e., incorrect responses on both first and second attempts) to two consecutive test items (excluding the two sample items). The brevity of this discontinue rule has been questioned, however it was set probabilistically and only about 5 percent of examinees would earn a higher scaled score if all examinees were given a discontinue rule of three consecutive 0-point responses as a ceiling.

### DON'T FORGET

On OIO, discontinue testing after only two consecutive 0-point responses.

## General Directions

A maximum of 30 seconds is allowed for examinees to begin their first response to each item. Record the examinee's response by circling the miniaturized figure or drawing on the RIST Record Form that corresponds to the figure or drawing the examinee pointed to on the picture card when responding to the item. If the examinee's response is correct on the first attempt, proceed to the next item. If the examinee's first attempt on an item is incorrect, a second attempt is allowed.

A maximum of 20 seconds is allowed for the examinee to begin his or her second attempt at the sample item. If the examinee's response is correct on the second attempt, proceed to the next item. If the examinee gives an incorrect response on his or her second attempt, score the item 0 and proceed to the next item.

### Scoring

On OIO, score 2 points for a correct response on the first attempt at a test item, and score 1 point for a correct response on the second attempt at a test item; an incorrect response on both attempts receives a score of 0. Indicate the examinee's score for a first response by circling either 0 or 2 in the space indicated on the RIST Record Form for each test item.

Give 2 points credit for every item below the basal level and 0 points for all items beyond the last item administered. The OIO total raw score is the sum of the raw scores obtained across all items (excluding the sample items).

**DON'T FORGET**

On OIO, if examinees do not get the item right on their first try, they get a second attempt.

### Obtaining Standard Scores

Raw scores for each subtest are converted to *T*-scores (Mean = 50, SD = 10) using tables in the RIST Manual (Reynolds & Kamphaus, 2003a). The RIST Composite Index (Mean = 100, SD =

**DON'T FORGET**

On OIO, a correct response to an item on the first try earns 2 points, while an incorrect response followed by a correct response on the second trial earns 1 point. An incorrect response on both trials earns a 0.

15) is obtained by summing the $T$-scores of the two subtests and entering this sum into a conversion table in the RIST Manual.

## INTERPRETATION

Although providing $T$-scores for highly reliable verbal and nonverbal components, the RIST composite score is recommended for virtually all purposes. The composite standard score is recommended because it is a widely understood metric, with a mean of 100 and a standard deviation of 15. In addition, as an interval scale of measurement, it is more appropriate for later statistical and evaluation studies of the screening process (e.g., receiver-operator characteristic curve analyses). The RIST Composite score can be described with a qualitative term as well to assist in conveying its meaning to others. Kamphaus (2001) suggested the adoption of the verbal scheme of Fish (1990) as a useful approach since Fish's scheme describes levels of performance without confounding this description with diagnostic terms that may force the examiner to provide awkward or unruly explanations later. The scheme in Table 3.6 thus is recommended by the RIST authors. Interpretation of the composite in a screening decision (i.e., to refer or not to refer for full evaluation) depends on the purpose of the evaluation. This issue has been discussed in detail in Chapter 1 of this work. Additional derived scores (normal curve equivalents, $z$-scores, etc.)

## Table 3.6  Recommended Qualitative Descriptors for the RIST Composite Index

| Verbal Descriptor | Intelligence Test Score Range |
| --- | --- |
| Significantly below average | $\leq 69$ |
| Moderately below average | 70–79 |
| Below average | 80–89 |
| Average | 90–109 |
| Above average | 110–119 |
| Moderately above average | 120–129 |
| Significantly above average | $\geq 130$ |

are offered for specialized assessment purposes that may be identified by RIST users.

In other settings, such as vocational screening or estimation of intellectual level in psychiatric or emotional and behavioral referrals, the RIST composite score can be interpreted pretty much as another summary IQ but with the knowledge that it is not confounded by fine motor skill, speed, or reading components, but also that it is a brief intelligence test and should not be used for diagnosis of cognitive disorders.

*≣ Rapid Reference 3.4*

## Strengths and Weaknesses of the RIST

### Strengths

- Extremely rapid and easy administration and scoring (8–12 minutes).
- Artwork is colorful and appealing.
- Assesses verbal and nonverbal dimensions.
- Covers an extensive age range of 3 years to 94 years.
- No fine motor tasks to confound assessment of intelligence.
- Practice items are provided for each subtest.
- Relatively pure measure of reasoning with few confounds.
- No bonus points or related speeded tasks.
- Wide range of scores available (i.e., composite scores from 40 to 160).

### Weaknesses

- Floor effects may appear at ages 3 and 4 years.
- Factor analytic data are not available due to small number of variables. Joint factor analyses with other tests might be useful and have not been done except with the RIAS.
- Two subtests may provide limited breadth of assessment.

*(continued)*

- Extensive review and statistical analyses to eliminate cultural biases both at the item level and test-score level.
- Standardization sample was large and closely matched U.S. Census data.
- Subtest and composite score reliabilities all above .90.
- Reliability coefficients are reported by age and separately by gender and ethnicity.
- Practice effects of repeated administration are very small allowing frequent readministration if necessary.
- Very high correlations with comprehensive measures of intelligence (e.g., RIAS, WISC-III, WAIS-III).

## 🐟 TEST YOURSELF 🐟

1. **The RIST contains two subtests that measure primarily** _____ **and** _____ **.**

   (a) general knowledge and recall

   (b) verbal reasoning and nonverbal reasoning

   (c) verbal memory and nonverbal memory

   (d) verbal reasoning and spatial skill

   (e) language development and mathematical reasoning

2. **RIST subtests are scaled to a mean of** _____ **and SD of** _____ **.**

   (a) 10, 3

   (b) 0, 1

   (c) 50, 10

   (d) 100, 15

   (e) 5, 2

3. **The RIST composite index is scaled to a mean of _____ and SD of _____.**

   (a)  10, 3

   (b)  100, 15

   (c)  100, 16

   (d)  50, 10

   (e)  50, 21.06

4. **RIST items were evaluated for cultural bias using which of the following methods?**

   (a)  ethnic minority psychologists as expert reviewers

   (b)  calculation of differential item functioning (DIF) statistics

   (c)  author reviews

   (d)  male and female psychologists

   (e)  all of the above

5. **To assist in designing a test with a rapid administration time, items were selected for the RIST _____.**

   (a)  that failed to show significant DIF

   (b)  that were either very easy or very hard

   (c)  to cover only a narrow range of IQs

   (d)  only if theoretically pure measures of a unidimensional construct

   (e)  that allowed development of a steep item difficulty gradient

6. **The RIST Manual provides supplementary score types for special purposes that include _____.**

   (a)  normal curve equivalents (NCEs)

   (b)  percentile ranks

   (c)  z-scores

   (d)  stanines

   (e)  all of the above

(continued)

**7. RIST standardized scores were calculated based upon a popular method known as _____.**

(a) continuous norming

(b) rolling weighted averages

(c) Pearson's curve fitting model

(d) hand-smoothing

(e) Lord's negative hypergeometric normal transformation

**8. The median internal consistency reliability coefficient for each RIST subtest and the composite index is best described as being _____.**

(a) .60 or higher

(b) .70 or higher

(c) .80 or higher

(d) .90 or higher

(e) .93 or higher

**9. The RIST composite index correlates with academic achievement test scores consistently in the range of about _____.**

(a) .40–.50

(b) .50–.60

(c) .60–.70

(d) .70–.80

(e) .80–.90

**10. The RIST computer scoring program _____.**

(a) allows raw score entry

(b) provides for unlimited test scoring and reporting

(c) has "cut and drop" features compatible with most major word processing programs

(d) will allow data export to most spreadsheet, database, statistical, and word processing programs

(e) all of the above

*Answers:* 1. b; 2. c; 3. b; 4. e; 5. e; 6. e; 7. a; 8. d; 9. c; 10. e

Four

# WECHSLER ABBREVIATED SCALE OF INTELLIGENCE (WASI)

The WASI is an individually administered intelligence test that was introduced in 1999. It was designed to be a short and reliable measure of estimated intelligence for use with individuals aged 6 to 89 years in clinical, psychoeducational, and research settings. The WASI is not intended to be a substitute for more comprehensive measures of intelligence and should not be used in isolation for diagnostic purposes or when making educational placement decisions. According to the *WASI Manual* (Psychological Corporation, 1999), this brief intelligence measure is appropriate for the following uses: (a) screening to determine if an in-depth evaluation using a comprehensive measure of intelligence is necessary; (b) retesting individuals—who received a more comprehensive evaluation using Wechsler scales at an earlier date—when time is limited; (c) obtaining estimates of IQs if an administration of a full battery is not possible due to time restraints (e.g., school, hospital, vocational, rehabilitation, research purposes); and (d) mass screening in settings such as schools, correctional facilities, or employment placement centers.

The WASI is nationally standardized and administration of the full battery yields Verbal, Performance, and Full Scale IQs. The four subtests of the WASI measure both fluid and crystallized intelligence, as well as verbal knowledge and nonverbal reasoning (Kaufman & Lichtenberger, 2006). The four subtests of the WASI include Vocabulary, Block Design,

Portions of this chapter are adapted with permission of the copyright holder, Harcourt Assessment, Inc., from The Psychological Corporation (1999), Wechsler Abbreviated Scale of Intelligence, San Antonio, TX: Harcourt Assessment, Inc.

# DON'T FORGET

The four-subtest version of the WASI that comprises the VIQ, PIQ, and FSIQ-4 can be administered in 30 minutes. The two-subtest form of the WAIS, consisting of Vocabulary and Matrix Reasoning, can be administered in approximately 15 minutes.

Similarities, and Matrix Reasoning. These four subtests compose the Full Scale and yield the Full Scale IQ (FSIQ-4). These subtests were chosen for their strong association with general cognitive abilities, or *g* (Psychological Corporation, 1999), and are similar in format to their counterpart subtests on the WISC-III and WAIS-III. The Vocabulary and Similarities subtests compose the Verbal Scale and yield the Verbal IQ (VIQ), and the Block Design and Matrix Reasoning subtests make up the Performance Scale and yield the Performance IQ (PIQ). The four subtests of the WASI that comprise an individual's verbal, nonverbal, and general cognitive functioning (FSIQ-4) can be administered in approximately 30 minutes. When time is a primary concern, the two-subtest form of the WASI, consisting of the Vocabulary and Matrix Reasoning subtests, may be administered in approximately 15 minutes. The two-subtest form of the WASI estimates general cognitive functioning and provides a Full Scale IQ (FSIQ-2); however, verbal and performance indices are not obtained. The two-subtest form is sufficient if the assessment requirement is a brief screening of an individual's cognitive functioning. For a description of the four WASI subtests, see Rapid Reference 4.1. The WASI is linked to the *Wechsler Intelligence Scale for Children–Third Edition* (WISC-III; Wechsler, 1991) and the *Wechsler Adult Intelligence Scale–Third Edition* (WAIS-III; Wechsler, 1997), and tables are provided for estimating IQ ranges on the WISC-III and the WAIS-III.

## STANDARDIZATION AND PSYCHOMETRIC PROPERTIES OF THE WASI

The standardization sample for the WASI ($N$ = 2,245) was selected according to the 1997 U.S. census data, and was stratified according to sex, race/ethnicity, educational level, and geographic region. Twenty-three

## Rapid Reference 4.1

### WASI Subtests

| Subtest | Description | Measures |
|---------|-------------|----------|
| Vocabulary | 42 items requiring the examinee to name picture items and provide oral definitions of words | fund of information, acquired knowledge, long-term memory, verbal expression |
| Similarities | 26 items requiring the examinee to choose which pictured objects share a common feature and explain how two common words are conceptually alike | acquired knowledge, verbal concept formation, verbal reasoning, abstract thinking |
| Block Design | 13 items requiring the examinee to use blocks to reconstruct visual patterns | visual-perceptual organization, visual problem-solving, motor coordination, fluid reasoning, processing speed |
| Matrix Reasoning | 35 items containing incomplete matrix patterns that the examinee completes by choosing from five possible choices | visual-perceptual organization, abstract reasoning, fluid reasoning |

age groups were created from a large sample of children, adolescents, and adults, with 75 to 100 subjects in each group between the ages of 6 and 89. Split-half and test-retest reliability coefficients were calculated for each of the WASI subtests, as well as for the IQ scales. To compute split-half reliabilities, the subtest items were divided into two subgroups and the two (half) tests were compared to demonstrate that there was no statistical significance between the halves. Overall, average reliability coefficients for the subtests and IQ indices are quite strong. For children aged 6 to 16, the average split-half reliability coefficients of the four WASI subtests

### ≣ Rapid Reference 4.2

## Wechsler Abbreviated Scale of Intelligence (WASI)

**Author:** The Psychological Corporation

**Publication date(s):** 1999

**What the test measures:** Verbal, nonverbal, and general intelligence

**Age range:** 6–89

**Administration time:** 4 subtests to obtain estimated VIQ, PIQ, and FSIQ = 30 minutes; 2 subtests to obtain estimated FSIQ only = 15 minutes or less

**Qualification of examiners:** Graduate- or professional-level training in psychological assessment

**Publisher:** The Psychological Corporation
555 Academic Court
San Antonio, TX 78204-2498
Ordering phone number: (800)-211-8378
http://www.PsychCorp.com

**Price** (as of May 2006): WASI Complete kit test price = $250.00

range from .87 to .92, while the average reliability coefficients for the VIQ, PIQ, and FSIQ-4 are .93, .94, and .96, respectively. Reliability coefficients for the FSIQ-2 for children range from .92 to .95, with an average of .93. For the adult sample aged 17 to 89, average reliability coefficients of the four WASI subtests range from .92 to .94. The average coefficients for the overall adult sample are .96, .96, and .98 for the VIQ, PIQ, and FSIQ-4, respectively. For adults, the reliability coefficients for the FSIQ-2 range from .93 to .98, with an average of .96.

The stability of scores on the WASI was assessed by using the test-retest method. Subjects were evaluated twice using the WASI within a period of 2 to 12 weeks, with an average test-retest interval of 31 days. Stability coefficients were calculated for four age bands: 6–11, 12–16, 17–54, and 55–89. For the child sample ($N = 116$), the average stability coefficients range from .77 to .86 for the subtests and from .88 to .93 for the IQ scales. For the adult sample ($N = 106$), the average stability coefficients range from .79 to .90 for the subtests and from .87 to .92 for the IQs. Stability coefficients for the FSIQ-2 are .85 and .88 for the child and adult samples, respectively. All of these coefficients are adequate for this type of reliability. As might be expected due to practice effects, scores of the second testing are consistently higher for both the subtests and the IQ scales and increases in the PIQ are higher than increases in the VIQ. See Table 4.1 for a list of split-half and test-retest reliabilities for the child and adult samples.

To gather evidence of convergent and discriminant validity of the WASI, three comparison studies are provided in the *WASI Manual* (Psychological Corporation, 1999) that investigate the relationship between the WASI and the WISC-III, the WAIS-III, and the *Wechsler Individual Achievement Test* (WIAT; Psychological Corporation, 1992). In 2003, the WISC-IV was published and a comparison study using the WASI and WISC-IV was made available (Wechsler, 2003). Results of the most recent study using the WASI and WISC-IV are provided here. The WASI and WISC-IV were administered in counterbalanced order to a nonclini-

## Table 4.1 Split-half and Test-retest Reliabilty of the WASI for Children and Adult Samples

| WASI Scale, Index, or Subtest | Children (ages 6–16) | | Adults (ages 17–89) | |
|---|---|---|---|---|
| | Split-Half Reliability | Test-Retest Reliability | Split-Half Reliability | Test-Retest Reliability |
| Verbal IQ | 0.93 | 0.92 | 0.96 | 0.92 |
| Performance IQ | 0.94 | 0.88 | 0.96 | 0.87 |
| Full Scale IQ-4 | 0.96 | 0.93 | 0.98 | 0.92 |
| Full Scale IQ-2 | 0.93 | 0.85 | 0.96 | 0.88 |
| Vocabulary | 0.89 | 0.85 | 0.94 | 0.90 |
| Similarities | 0.87 | 0.86 | 0.92 | 0.88 |
| Block Design | 0.90 | 0.81 | 0.92 | 0.86 |
| Matrix Reasoning | 0.92 | 0.77 | 0.94 | 0.79 |

Test-retest reliability correlations were corrected for restriction of range (Guilford & Fruchter, 1978).

cal sample of 260 children and adolescents aged 6 to 16 years (M = 11.4, SD = 3.0). The testing interval between the two administrations ranged from 12 to 64 days, with a mean of 29 days. Correlation coefficients are .77, .73, .79, and .71 for Block Design, Similarities, Vocabulary, and Matrix Reasoning subtests, respectively. Coefficients for the IQ scales are .85, .78, and .86 for the VIQ/VCI, PIQ/PRI, and FSIQ-4/ FSIQ. The correlation coefficient between the WASI FSIQ-2 and the WISC-IV FSIQ was .83. Results suggest that the subtests and IQ of the WASI correlate moderately well with their WISC-IV counterparts. Table 4.2 reports the mean scores, standard deviations, and correlation coefficients between the IQ and subtest scores on the WASI and WISC-IV (Wechsler, 2003, Table 5.14, p. 68).

## Table 4.2 Correlations Between the WASI and the WISC-IV

| Subtest/Composite | WASI | | WISC-IV | | |
| | T-Score | | | | |
| | Mean[a] | SD | Mean[a] | SD | $r_{12}$[b] |
|---|---|---|---|---|---|
| Block Design | 53.0 | 10.6 | 10.4 | 3.1 | .77 |
| Similarities | 52.3 | 10.5 | 10.0 | 2.9 | .73 |
| Vocabulary | 50.4 | 10.1 | 9.9 | 3.0 | .79 |
| Matrix Reasoning | 51.4 | 10.2 | 10.3 | 3.1 | .71 |
| VIQ-VCI | 102.6 | 15.1 | 98.9 | 14.4 | .85 |
| PIQ-PRI | 104.0 | 15.3 | 101.4 | 14.5 | .78 |
| WMI | | | 100.7 | 14.4 | |
| PSI | | | 98.4 | 13.7 | |
| FSIQ-4 | 103.6 | 15.1 | 100.2 | 14.8 | .86 |
| FSIQ-2 | 102.0 | 14.5 | 100.2 | 14.8 | .83 |

*Note.* N = 260. Correlations were computed separately for each order of administration in a counterbalanced design and corrected for the variability of the WISC-IV standardization sample (Guilford & Fruchter, 1978).

[a] The values in the Mean columns are the average of the means of the two administration orders.

[b] The weighted average across both administration orders was obtained with Fisher's $z$ transformation.

Results of the comparison study using the WASI and WISC-III are similar to that of the WASI and WISC-IV and are available in the *WASI Manual* (Psychological Corporation, 1999, Table 5.5, p. 134).

In a similar study, the WASI and WAIS-III were administered in counterbalanced order to a sample of 248 adults aged 16 to 89 years (M = 51.98, SD = 23.48). The testing interval between the two administrations was 2 to 12 weeks (M = 28 days, SD = 14 days). Correlation coefficients between the WASI and WAIS-III Vocabulary, Similarities, Block Design, and Matrix Reasoning subtests are .88, .76, .83, and .66, respectively. The VIQ, PIQ, and FSIQ-4 correlation coefficients are .88, .84, and .92. The correlation coefficient is .87 between the WASI FSIQ-2 and the WAIS-III FSIQ. Table 4.3 reports the mean scores, standard deviations, and

**Table 4.3  Correlations Between the WASI and the WAIS-III**

| Subtest/Scale | WASI | | | WAIS-III | | |
| | *T*-Score | | Scaled Score | | | |
| | Mean[a] | SD | Equivalent[b] | Mean[a] | SD | $r_{12}$[c] |
|---|---|---|---|---|---|---|
| Vocabulary | 52.3 | 10.5 | 10.7 | 10.8 | 3.1 | 0.88 |
| Similarities | 52.4 | 10.3 | 10.7 | 10.8 | 3.0 | 0.76 |
| Block Design | 52.0 | 10.2 | 10.6 | 10.6 | 3.2 | 0.83 |
| Matrix Reasoning | 51.2 | 10.1 | 10.4 | 10.7 | 3.1 | 0.66 |
| VIQ | 104.1 | 15.2 | | 103.8 | 15.4 | 0.88 |
| PIQ | 102.8 | 14.5 | | 102.6 | 15.4 | 0.84 |
| FSIQ-4 | 104.0 | 14.7 | | 103.6 | 15.5 | 0.92 |
| FSIQ-2 | 103.5 | 14.5 | | 103.6 | 15.5 | 0.87 |

*Note.* N = 248. Correlations were computed separately for each order of administration in a counterbalanced design and corrected for restriction of range (Guilford & Fruchter, 1978).

[a] The values in the Mean columns are the average of the means of the two administration orders.

[b] The scaled-score equivalents of the WASI subtest *T*-scores are based on the data provided in Table A.2 of the *WASI Manual*.

[c] The weighted average was obtained with Fisher's $z$ transformation.

correlation coefficients between the IQ and subtest scores on WASI and the WISC-III and WAIS-III (Psychological Corporation, 1999, Table 5.6, p. 136).

As with the WISC-III and WAIS-III, the WASI correlated moderately with the WIAT subtest scores. Correlations with Reading Comprehension, Math Reasoning, and Basic Reading ranged from the .50s to .70s. Correlations with Oral Expression are in the .40s. The WASI IQs and WIAT composite score correlations are moderate to high, ranging from .53 to .72.

## ADMINISTRATION AND SCORING POINTERS

Rules for administering each of the four WASI subtests are presented in the manual. In this section we present important reminders for competent administration of each subtest. This section will be especially useful to new users of the test but may also refresh your memory if you have already learned the details of test administration. We review the two Verbal subtests and two Performance subtests for the WASI. Because obtaining detailed behavior observations during testing may give insight into how to interpret an individual's subtest score, we identify key behaviors that you will want to watch for.

### Vocabulary

Administration of the Vocabulary subtest of the WASI requires the stimulus book plus the manual and record form. The first four items of the WASI Vocabulary subtest are pictures that the examinee is required to name. If the examinee does not correctly name the picture on items 1 or 2, give the examinee the correct answer. Do not provide assistance for the remaining items on this subtest. WASI Vocabulary items 5 through 42 are words that the examiner reads aloud and the examinee is asked to define. For examinees aged 9 to 89, point to each word in the stimulus booklet as you pronounce it so that the examinee can read along. For examinees aged 6 to 8, however, do not use the stimulus booklet for items 5 through 42.

For all examinees, read aloud each question verbatim. With more able examinees, you may simply pronounce each word after the administration of the first three verbal items (items 5–42). Be sure to use the local pronunciation of each word or the pronunciation that you believe to be familiar to the examinee. Rapid Reference 4.3 reviews the start, reverse, discontinue, stop, and timing rules.

Scoring should be completed as responses are recorded to the degree possible. It is best to continue administering items if you are unsure if a difficult-to-score response will affect the discontinue rule. Recording the

## *Rapid Reference 4.3*

### Summary of Vocabulary Rules

**Starting Points**

Ages 6–8: Item 5

Ages 9–89: Item 9

**Reverse Criterion**

Ages 6–8: Score of 0 or 1 on either Item 5 or 6, administer items 1–4 in *forward* sequence

Ages 9–89: Score of 0 or 1 on either Item 9 or 10, administer items 5–8 in *reverse* sequence until examinee obtains perfect scores on two consecutive items

**Discontinue Criterion**

After five consecutive scores of 0

**Stop Criterion**

Ages 6–8: After item 30

Ages 9–11: After item 34

Ages 12–16: After item 38

Ages 17–89: No stop point

**Timing**

Not timed

exact response of the examinee will assist with scoring when it is necessary to review responses after the test is over. Sample responses are listed in the manual for 0-, 1-, and 2-point responses; however, responses are illustrative only and are by no means exhaustive. Occasionally, the examinee's response may be unclear or too vague to be readily scored or is followed by a "(Q)" in the sample responses provided in the manual. In these cases, query the response by saying, "Tell me more about it," or "Explain what you mean," or make a similarly neutral inquiry. In some instances, sample responses provided in the *WASI Manual* contain alternative words or phrases in parentheses, all followed by a "(Q)." In this instance, all of the responses must be queried. For example, any of the three responses indicated by "It has thick fur (four legs, a tail) (Q)" must be queried. Some sample responses have a "(Q)" within the response followed by a dash and additional words, for example, "A fruit (Q)—that grows on trees and has seeds." The part of the response preceding the "(Q)" is the examinee's spontaneous response that must be queried. The part of the response following the dash is the examinee's elaboration after the query, which is required to earn more credit.

If a response is clearly a 0- or 1-point response, querying is inappropriate. Use the general distinctions between responses scored 2, 1, and 0 provided on pages 84 and 85 of *WASI Manual*. If an examinee provides a 2- or 1-point response to an item but also includes a spoiled response, he or she earns no credit. If the examinee provides several responses that vary greatly in quality, none of which is spoiled, score the best response. Discontinue after five consecutive scores of 0. If the discontinue criterion has not been met, discontinue *after* the stop item specified for the examinee's age group.

There are no stringent time limits for the WASI Vocabulary subtest. However, you should not allow the examinee more than approximately 30 seconds to respond to each item. If the examinee has not responded after 30 seconds, count the item as a failure and proceed to the next item. Rapid Reference 4.4 notes behaviors to watch for when administering this subtest.

## ≡ Rapid Reference 4.4

### Behaviors to Note on Vocabulary

- Make note of "I don't know" responses, as this response may be indicative of children or adults with word retrieval problems. Word fluency can impact an individual's performance as much as his or her word knowledge.

- Hearing difficulties may be apparent on the WASI Vocabulary test. Although items are presented in oral and written formats for individuals aged 9 to 89, the Vocabulary words are not presented in a meaningful context. Hearing problems may be more apparent on the Vocabulary subtest for children with reading problems, or illiterate or dyslexic adults. Note behaviors such as leaning forward during administration to hear. It also is important to watch for indications of auditory discrimination problems (defining "confine" rather than "confide").

- Note children or adults who are overly verbose in their responses. They may be anxious regarding their test performance, obsessive, or inefficient in their verbal expression.

- Some individuals may jump ahead and proceed with visually presented words before the examiner has said the word aloud. Such behavior may indicate that the examinee has a preference for visual rather than auditory stimuli. The examinee may also exhibit an impulsive response style.

### Similarities

Materials needed to administer the WASI Similarities subtest include the stimulus booklet, manual, and record form. For items 1 through 4, the examinee is presented with a page from the stimulus booklet that has two rows of pictures (three pictures on the top and four pictures on the bottom). The examinee must identify the picture in the bottom row that is most similar to the pictures in the top row. Feedback is provided on item one to all examinees who are administered the item by giving the encouragement or help specified in the instructions. The stimulus booklet is not used for WASI Similarities items 5 through 26. For these items, the examinee is read two words that represent common concepts or objects. The examinee is required to state how the two objects or concepts are alike. For ages 6 to 8 and 9 to 11, if the examinee gives a 1- or 0-point response on item 5, feedback is provided; for ages 12 to 89, if the examinee gives a 1- or 0-point response on item 7, provide feedback to the examinee. By providing an example of a 2-point response on these items, the examinee is provided with the opportunity to hear a response with a higher degree of abstraction than a purely concrete answer.

When working with more able examinees, the examiner may omit the formal question after the administration of the first three items. The examiner may simply pronounce the pair of stimulus words in isolation. Rapid Reference 4.5 reviews the start, reverse, discontinue, stop, and timing rules for the Similarities subtest.

Consistent with administration of the WASI Vocabulary subtest, it is important to carefully record the verbal responses. Examiners need to be aware of what types of responses need to be queried (those that are unclear or vague and those specifically listed in the manual). In such cases, use the queries, "What do you mean?" or "Tell me more about it," or a similarly neutral inquiry. Be sure to record a *Q* on the record form after a queried response. Because it is important to score as you administer items, examiners need to be familiar with the scoring principles for items 5 through 26, listed on pages 116 and 117 of *WASI Manual,* before administering the subtest.

As with the Vocabulary subtest, if the examinee provides multiple responses for an item that vary greatly in quality, none of which is spoiled, score the best response. If the examinee provides a 2- or 1-point response to an item but also includes a spoiled response, score the item as 0. Discontinue after

## DON'T FORGET

For the Vocabulary, Similarities, and Matrix Reasoning subtests, if the discontinue criterion has not previously been met, discontinue immediately *after* the stop item specified in the examinee's age group.

≡ *Rapid Reference 4.5*

### Summary of Similarities Rules

**Starting Points**

Ages 6–8: Item 1

Ages 9–11: Item 5

Ages 12–89: Item 7

**Reverse Criterion**

Ages 9–89: Score of 0 or 1 on either Item 5 or 6, administer items 1–4 in *forward* sequence

Ages 12–89: Score of 0 or 1 on either Item 7 or 8, administer items 5 and 6 in *reverse* sequence until examinee obtains perfect scores on two consecutive items

**Discontinue Criterion**

After four consecutive scores of 0

**Stop Criterion**

Ages 6–8: After item 20

Ages 9–11: After item 24

Ages 12–89: No stop point

**Timing**

Not timed

four consecutive scores of 0. If the discontinue criterion has not been met, discontinue *after* the stop item specified for the examinee's age group.

There is not a strict time limit for the WASI Similarities subtest; however, if the examinee has not responded after 30 seconds, the examiner should count the item as a failure and proceed with the next item of the subtest. Rapid Reference 4.6 reviews behaviors to watch for and note while administering this subtest.

≡ *Rapid Reference 4.6*

## Behaviors to Note on Similarities

- Make note of whether the child or adult benefits from feedback on items 1, 5, and 7 (if feedback is given). Individuals who learn from examples may be flexible in their thinking, whereas those who cannot may be more concrete.
- Observe whether the individual has particular difficulty with the visual items 1 through 4 (if administered) in comparison to the auditory items. This could be indicative of visual processing difficulties.
- Be aware of how an examinee deals with frustration on this task as items become more difficult. For example, a response of "They are not alike," may indicate avoidance or defensiveness. Other individuals may give up when faced with difficult items and simply respond with "I don't know."
- Make note of whether the quality of responses decreases as the items become more difficult.
- Overly verbose responses may suggest anxiety, word finding difficulties, or obsessiveness.
- Quick, automatic responses may indicate overlearned associations rather than abstract reasoning.

### Block Design

Assuming the examinee has no motor coordination or motor speed problems, the WASI Block Design subtest evaluates the ability to understand two- and three-dimensional representations. In the first three designs, the examiner provides a model that is three-dimensional that the examinee then replicates in three-dimensional space. As the subtest becomes more complex (designs 4–13), the examinee is required to look at two-dimensional design shown in the stimulus book and replicate it in three-dimensional space. On more difficult items, some of the visual cues are removed. For example, on later items the outline of the models is not visible.

The WASI Block Design subtest requires several materials including the box of nine blocks, stimulus booklet with model forms, stopwatch, administration manual, and record form. The examinee, blocks, and stimulus booklet must be positioned correctly to ensure proper administration (see Figure 4.1 on page 88 of *WASI Manual*). To prevent the examinee from looking at

> **DON'T FORGET**
> ....................................................
> Block Design items can be failed because of faulty construction, rotation of 30 degrees or more, or exceeding the time limit.

the sides instead of the top of the block design on Designs 1 through 3, place the model in front of the examinee so that he or she is required to look down on it approximately 7 inches from the edge of the table closest to him or her. If the examinee is right-handed, the model should be placed a little to the left of a line perpendicular to his or her body; conversely, the model should be placed a little to the right if the examinee is left-handed.

Designs 1 through 4 are modeled by the examiner and replicated by the examinee. Designs 1 through 4 each contain two trials; only administer the second trial if the examinee did not successfully construct the design within the time limit. For items 4 through 13, the examinee replicates the design models shown in the stimulus booklet. A design can be failed because of faulty construction, rotation of 30 degrees or more, or exceeding the time limit. For designs 5 through 13, the examinee can earn 1 to 3 bonus points per design for a speedy, perfect performance. For each item, record the completion time in seconds, indicate whether the design was correctly constructed by circling the "Y" for yes or the "N" for no, circle the appropriate score, and draw the incorrect design, if applicable. Rapid Reference 4.7 reviews the start, reverse, discontinue, stop, and timing rules. Following is a list of important WASI Block Design rules to note while administering this subtest. Rapid Reference 4.8 reviews behaviors to watch for while administering this subtest.

### WASI Block Design Rules
- Begin timing after the last word of instructions.
- Blocks must have a variety of faces showing before each administration; for a four-block design, only one block should have a

## ≡ *Rapid Reference 4.7*

### Summary of Block Design Rules

**Starting Points**

Ages 6–8: Item 1

Ages 9–89: Item 3

**Reverse Criterion**

Ages 9–89: Score of 0 or 1 on Designs 3 or Design 4, administer Designs 1–2 in *reverse* sequence until examinee obtains perfect scores on two consecutive items

**Discontinue Criterion**

After three consecutive scores of 0

**Stop Criterion**

All Ages: No stop point

**Timing**

30 seconds for Design 1

60 seconds for Designs 2–9

120 seconds for Designs 10–13

---

red-and-white side facing up. For a nine-block design, only three blocks should have a red-and-white side facing up. If a variety of block faces are displayed, the level of difficulty is consistent across items.

- Rotation of a design by 30 degrees or more is considered a failure. Only one rotation can be corrected during the entire administration of the subtest.
- Provide the extra blocks and appropriate directions for Designs 10 through 13.
- Do not permit the examinee to rotate the stimulus booklet.
- If examinee indicates that he or she has finished a design and then spontaneously changes the design, give credit if modifications were made within the specified time limit.

## ≡ Rapid Reference 4.8

### Behaviors to Note on Block Design

• Make note of the examinee's level of planning. Does the examinee formulate a plan before reconstructing the designs or does he or she start the task impulsively?

• Observe the child or adult's problem-solving style. While some use a trial-and-error approach, others will use a random, haphazard style to manipulate the blocks. Note whether examinees start on the outside and work in or whether they "chunk" two or three blocks together and then piece the "chunks" together to construct the design.

• Sometimes examinees will re-create an overall pattern but lose the square shape of the design. This pattern of performance may be indicative of figure-ground problems.

• Look to see whether examinees look back to models repeatedly while they are working. This could indicate visual memory problems, anxiety, or cautiousness.

• Make note of the level of motor coordination used on this task. For example, do examinees use one or both hands to construct design? Note whether motor control appears steady and quick or clumsy and slow.

• Note whether examinees tend to be obsessively concerned with lining up the blocks. This behavior may negatively impact speed and adversely affect his or her overall scaled score.

• Observe how examinees respond when the task becomes more difficult and they face frustration. Do they persist and keep on working even past the time limit or give up easily after a single failed attempt?

• Make note of whether examinees fail to recognize that their designs look different from the models. Such behaviors may indicate visual-perceptual difficulties.

---

• Record completion time, indicate whether or not the design was correctly constructed (circle "Y" for yes and "N" for no), circle the appropriate score, and document incorrect responses by drawing the block construction in the designated area of the record form.

## DON'T FORGET

If the examinee does not provide a response on the Matrix Reasoning subtest after 30 seconds have elapsed, count the item as a failure. However, do not abruptly stop an examinee if he or she is about to give a response even after 30 seconds have elapsed.

### Matrix Reasoning

The stimulus booklet, the record form, and the administration manual are necessary to administer the WASI Matrix Reasoning subtest. Sample items A and B are teaching items and are administered to all examinees to ensure that they understand the task. If the child or adult fails a sample item, the examiner teaches the task using the standardized directions provided in the administration manual. The examiner may teach the task via alternative explanation on sample item A if the child or adult does not understand the reasoning behind the task. Do not provide an alternative explanation on sample item B. Regardless of performance on sample items, proceed to the appropriate start item. Rapid Reference 4.9 reviews start, reverse, discontinue, stop, and timing rules.

There is no rigid time limit on this subtest; however, if the examinee has not provided a response after approximately 30 seconds, count the item as a failure and move on to the next item. Do not abruptly stop the child or adult if he or she is about to give a response, even after approximately 30 seconds has elapsed. Allow the examinee to respond and give credit if the response is correct. No teaching or feedback should be given on items 1 through 35. Point correctly to the response options and the empty box in the stimulus booklet. The types of behaviors that may be important to observe during administration of this subtest are listed in Rapid Reference 4.10.

## SCORING THE WASI

Administration of the WASI results in three types of scores called raw scores, *T*-scores, and IQs. The first score the examiner computes is the raw score,

*≡ Rapid Reference 4.9*

## Summary of Matrix Reasoning Rules

### Starting Points

Ages 6–8: Sample Items A & B and then Item 1

Ages 9–11: Sample Items A & B and then Item 5

Ages 12–44: Sample Items A & B and then Item 7

Ages 45–79: Sample Items A & B and then Item 5

Ages 80–89: Sample Items A & B and then Item 1

### Reverse Criterion

Ages 9–11: Score of 0 on Item 5 or 6, administer Items 1–4 in *reverse* sequence until examinee obtains perfect scores on two consecutive items

Ages 12–44: Score of 0 on Item 7 or 8, administer Items 1–6 in *reverse* sequence until examinee obtains perfect scores on two consecutive items

Ages 45–79: Score of 0 on Item 5 or 6, administer Items 1–4 in *reverse* sequence until examinee obtains perfect scores on two consecutive items

### Discontinue Criterion

After four consecutive scores of 0 or four scores of 0 on five consecutive items

### Stop Criterion

Ages 6–8: After Item 28

Ages 9–11: After Item 32

Ages 12–44: No stop point

Ages 45–79: After Item 32

Ages 80–89: After Item 28

### Timing

Not timed

## ≡ Rapid Reference 4.10

### Behaviors to Note on Matrix Reasoning

- There are several problem-solving approaches that examinees may adopt. Observe whether the child or adult attempts to first come up with a possible solution and then looks for that solution among the response choices. If this is not the case, does the examinee try each of the possible solutions one by one?
- Although the test is not timed, make note of how long it takes the examinee to process information.
- Observe whether examinees use strategies such as talking their way through the problem in order to work to a solution.
- Note whether the subject attends to some of the details of the matrix but misses other essential parts to successfully complete the design.
- Observe how the individual responds to stimuli as designs become increasingly complex. Watch for signs of anxiety and frustration. Does the examinee persist on difficult items or quickly give up?

which is simply the total number of points earned on a single subtest. In order to be norm-referenced, a raw score must then be converted into a standard score (*T*-score, IQ). The various metrics for each type of WASI standard score are listed in Rapid Reference 4.11. Individual subtests produce *T*-scores with a mean of 50 and a standard deviation of 10 (ranging from 20 to 80 for all subtests). The IQs have a mean of 100 and standard deviation of 15. The range of IQs differs slightly across WASI indices (Verbal IQ = 55–156; Performance IQ = 53–157; FSIQ-4 = 50–160; and FSIQ-2 = 55–157).

## DON'T FORGET

WASI subtest raw scores are converted to *T*-scores instead of subtest scaled scores.

### *T*-scores

The WASI differs from other Wechsler scales in that subtest total raw scores are converted to *T*-scores instead of subtest scaled

## ≡ Rapid Reference 4.11

### Metrics for Standard Scores on the WASI

| Type of Standard Score | Mean | SD | Range of Values |
|---|---|---|---|
| T-score | 50 | 10 | 20–80 |
| Verbal IQ | 100 | 15 | 55–156 |
| Performance IQ | 100 | 15 | 53–157 |
| FSIQ-4 | 100 | 15 | 50–160 |
| FSIQ-2 | 100 | 15 | 55–157 |

### CAUTION

### Common Errors in Obtaining Standard Scores

- miscalculating the chronological age, which leads to referencing the wrong age group
- errors encountered when adding numbers to obtain the raw score or the sum of scaled scores
- errors that occur when transferring sum of raw score from the inside of the record form to front cover
- using a score conversion table for the wrong age group
- misreading across the rows of score-conversion tables
- writing illegibly, which leads to errors

scores. According to the *WASI Manual* (Psychological Corporation, 1999), the *T*-score scale is used because it has a wider range of score points and can better differentiate the levels of ability reflected by the subtest total raw scores. Converting the raw scores obtained on the WASI to *T*-scores is relatively simple. The examiner will need the following information: (a) the individual's chronological age, (b) the individual's raw scores on all subtests, and (c) Table A.1 from the *WASI Manual* (Psychological Cor-

## ≡ Rapid Reference 4.12

### James G. (32-year-old male) Wechsler Abbreviated Scale of Intelligence (WASI) Profile

| Scale | IQ | 90% Confidence Interval | Percentile Rank |
|---|---|---|---|
| Verbal Scale | 119 | 113–123 | 90 |
| Performance Scale | 86 | 82–91 | 18 |
| Full Scale IQ-4 | 102 | 99–105 | 55 |

| Subtest | T-Score | Scaled Score | Subtest | T-Score | Scaled Score |
|---|---|---|---|---|---|
| Vocabulary | 69 | 15 | Block Design | 40 | 7 |
| Similarities | 61 | 13 | Matrix Reasoning | 41 | 7 |

poration, 1999, pp. 160–82). The following list of steps outlines the process of converting raw scores to *T*-scores.

1. Using the space provided on the front right-hand corner of the WASI record form, calculate the individual's chronological age.
2. Next, transfer the raw scores from the inside of the record form to the front cover. The subtests on the cover of the record form are listed in administration order.
3. Look up the examinee's raw score and its corresponding *T*-score equivalent in Table A.1 for each WASI subtest administered. For individuals who are ages 6 to 16 years, norms are provided for each 4-month age span. For individuals who are ages 17 to 89, norms are provided by various age groups. The individual's age in years, months, and days determines which section of Table A.1 to use. For each subtest, find the raw score in the column

## ≡ Rapid Reference 4.13

### WASI Full Scale IQ-4 Qualitative Interpretation

| | | Percent Included | |
| | | Theoretical | Actual |
| IQ Score | Classification | Normal Curve | Sample |
|---|---|---|---|
| 130 and above | Very Superior | 2.2 | 2.0 |
| 120–129 | Superior | 6.7 | 7.3 |
| 110–119 | High Average | 16.1 | 15.6 |
| 90–109 | Average | 50.0 | 50.0 |
| 80–89 | Low Average | 16.1 | 15.8 |
| 70–79 | Borderline | 6.7 | 6.8 |
| 69 and below | Extremely Low | 2.2 | 2.5 |

The percentages shown are for the FSIQ-4 and are based on the total standardization sample ($N$ = 2,245).

under the subtest name. Read across to the left or right to find the corresponding $T$-score.

4. Enter the $T$-score in the $T$-score column on the cover page of the record form. If all four subtests of the WASI were administered, the Vocabulary and Similarity $T$-scores should be recorded in the first column of $T$-scores and the Block Design and Matrix Reasoning $T$-scores are indicated in the second column of $T$-scores. If only the two-subtest version of the WASI was administered, enter the Vocabulary and Matrix Reasoning $T$-scores in the third column of boxes provided for $T$-scores.

5. To facilitate interpretation, a graph is provided on the record form for plotting the WASI subtest $T$-scores. To plot a score, simply place a dot on the point in the graph that corresponds to

the value in the column labeled for that score. Examiners may choose to place bars at the lower and upper ranges to reflect the confidence interval for that score.

## IQ

Obtaining IQs is the next step in the process of test-score conversion. The following steps outline how to convert T-scores to IQs and should be carefully followed to obtain accurate indices.

1. If all 4 subtests were administered, calculate the sum of T-scores for the Verbal and Performance scores. Record the scores in the boxes at the bottom of the corresponding T-score columns on the record form.

2. Add the Verbal and Performance scales' sums of T-scores to obtain the Full Scale score (FSIQ-4). Record the score in the appropriate box under the sums of Verbal and Performance T-scores. If the two-subtest version of the WASI was administered, add the T-scores for the Vocabulary and Similarities subtests to obtain the Full Scale score (FSIQ-2). Record the score in the box provided on the record form.

3. Transfer the sums of T-scores for the Verbal, Performance, and the Full Scale-4 (or Full Scale-2) scores to the IQ section on the lower left-hand corner of the front of the record form. Next, determine the appropriate IQ based on the sum of T-scores. See Tables A.3–A.6, respectively, for the Verbal IQ, Performance IQ, four-subtest Full Scale IQ, and two-subtest Full Scale IQ (Psychological Corporation, 1999, pp. 184–93). Record the values in the appropriate boxes on the record form.

4. Record the percentile ranks and confidence intervals for each of the scales. They are found in Tables A.3 to A.6 of the *WASI Manual* (Psychological Corporation, 1999). Note that the 90 per-

cent and 95 percent confidence intervals are provided separately
for children and adults.

5. To assist with interpretation, a graph is provided on the record
   form for plotting the WASI subtest IQ. IQs may be plotted for
   the VIQ, PIQ, FSIQ-4, and FSIQ-2.

## Prediction Intervals of Full-Battery FSIQs

The WASI was linked to the WISC-III and WAIS-III during standardization to ensure the equivalency of Wechsler measures. As a result, prediction intervals of the WISC-III and WAIS-III FSIQ based on WASI
FSIQ-4 scores can be determined by adhering to the steps outlined in
the following. Prediction intervals of the WISC-III and WAIS-III are not
provided for the FSIQ-2 scores.

1. Depending on the age of the individual tested, determine the
   prediction intervals. For ages 6 to 16, Table B.1 (Psychological
   Corporation, 1999, p. 196) provides prediction intervals for the
   WISC-III FSIQ. For ages 16 to 89, Table B.2 (p. 197) provides
   prediction intervals for the WAIS-III FSIQ.
2. In the left column of Table B.1 or B.2 (depending on the examinee's age), locate the individual's obtained WASI FSIQ-4 score.
   Following the score to the right, find the full-battery FSIQ
   prediction intervals at the 90 percent and 68 percent levels of
   confidence.
3. Record the prediction interval in the appropriate boxes in the
   IQ Scores section of the record form.

## Special Considerations for IQs with Subtest Raw Scores of Zero

Subtest raw scores of zero deserve special attention when being converted
to T-scores and IQs. It would be unlikely to encounter a raw score of zero

# DON'T FORGET

A raw score of zero on a subtest does not indicate that the examinee lacks a particular ability, but it does mean that the subtest did not have enough of the easier items necessary to evaluate the individual's skills.

when testing adults due to the low floor items; however, this problem may occur when evaluating children. The problem with a raw score of zero is that you cannot determine the individual's true ability to perform on the subtest. A zero raw score does not indicate that the examinee lacks a particular ability, but it does mean that the subtest did not have enough of the easier floor items to adequately evaluate the individual's skills. If the examinee obtains a raw score of zero on the Vocabulary or Similarities subtests of the WASI, the Verbal IQ and FSIQ-4 should not be computed. Likewise, if a raw score of zero is present on either the Block Design or Matrix Reasoning subtests, the Performance IQ and FSIQ-4 should not be computed. If a raw score of zero is obtained on either the Vocabulary or Matrix Reasoning subtests of the two-subtest version of the WASI, a FSIQ-2 should not be computed.

## Scoring Subtests Requiring Judgment

Consistent with administration of other Wechsler instruments, you will likely find that examinees provide many more responses to Verbal subtest items than what are listed in the manual. The *WASI Manual* provides scoring criteria and sample responses for the Vocabulary and Similarities subtests. Unfortunately, it is impossible to list every possible answer that an examinee may provide; therefore, it is left up to the examiner to interpret the scoring system for each of the unique responses.

Examinees will frequently provide an answer that appears to be better than a 1-point response but is not quite sufficient to earn 2 points; borderline responses are the ones likely to present the greatest scoring difficulty.

Because it is not possible to score responses with a 1.5, examiners must have good judgment in deciding how to score a response. It is important to familiarize yourself with scoring examples and have a clear understanding of the general scoring criteria in the *WASI Manual*. General scoring principles for the Vocabulary and Similarities subtests are outlined on pages 84 to 86 and 116 to 117 of the *WASI Manual*, respectively.

There are several rules to keep in mind when scoring verbal responses. First, examinees should not be penalized for poor grammar or improper pronunciation of words. While it is important to make clinical observations when poor grammar or improper pronunciation occurs, it is the content of responses that is of most importance when scoring items. Second, if a response is queried, the examinee's reply to the query is evaluated as part of the entire response. If the elaboration improves the response, change the score accordingly. If the elaboration does not improve the response, the score remains the same, even if the elaboration is of lesser quality than the spontaneous response. If an examinee's response after a query demonstrates a fundamental misconception of the item, award 0 points for the item because the examinee's elaboration spoiled the response.

Some individuals have a tendency to provide long, verbose responses that might contain two or three different answers. If this occurs, either immediately following the question or after a query, it is the examiner's responsibility to determine whether the response is spoiled, which part of the response was intended as the final response, and which part of the response is worth the highest number of points. If the examinee reveals a fundamental misconception in his or her lengthy and elaborate response, then the entire response is spoiled and the item is scored as zero. Sometimes the examinee clearly indicates that the last answer provided is intended to be the actual response. If this is the case, score the last response. At other times it is unclear which response is intended as the actual response. In such a case, ask the examinee to clarify his or her response by asking, "Which is it, _____ or _____?" Some examinees may say that the entire response was what they intended the answer to be, and embedded in that lengthy response are 0-, 1-, and 2-point responses. In this case, if no answer spoils the response, then simply score the best response.

## SUBTEST-BY-SUBTEST SCORING KEYS

The following section lists important pointers to remember when scoring each of the four WASI subtests. Listed are areas that commonly cause scoring difficulties for examiners.

### Vocabulary

- Items 1 through 4 of WASI Vocabulary are worth 0 to 1 point each, while the remaining WASI items are worth 0, 1, or 2 points.
- Add appropriate number of points to the raw score for each of the unadministered reversal items.
- Poor grammar and improper pronunciation are not penalized in scoring.
- Any meaning found in a standard dictionary is given credit.
- Slang and regionalisms not in the dictionary are scored as 0.
- Use specific examples and the general scoring criteria provided in the *WASI Manual*.

### Similarities

- The key to scoring is based on the degree of abstraction and pertinence.
- WASI Similarities items 1 through 4 are worth either 0 or 1 point each, and the remaining WASI items are worth 0, 1, or 2 points each.
- For Similarities items 5 through 26, use the general 0- to 2-point scoring criteria and specific examples.

### Block Design

- Block Design scoring is based on the correctness of the design and completion time.

- For Block Design items 1 through 4, the successful completion on the first trial within the time limit earns 2 points while successful completion on the second trial within the time limit earns 1 point.
- For examinees aged 9 to 89 who obtain full credit on Designs 3 and 4, award 2 points each for Designs 1 and 2.
- For Designs 5 through 13, the examinee can earn 1 to 3 bonus points per design for quick, perfect performance.
- No credit is given for partially completed designs.

## *Matrix Reasoning*
- Do not add score from Sample Items A and B into calculation of the raw score.
- Add one point to the raw score for each of the unadministered reversal items.
- The correct answers are displayed in bold font on the record form.
- Because this is not a timed subtest, examinees are not penalized for slow performance.

## Step 1. Interpret the WASI Full Scale IQ-4 and Full Scale IQ-2

Of the scores provided by the WASI, the Full Scale IQ-4 is the most reliable score (average split-half for children and adults, respectively [$r$ = .96, $r$ = .98]; average test-retest for children and adults, respectively [$r$ = .93, $r$ = .92]). This is the most global score and should be clearly communicated in the interpretive report if it is the best estimate of the individual's abilities. Along with the Full Scale IQ-4, the confidence interval, percentile rank, and descriptive category should be indicated. Although the interpretive process begins with the Full Scale IQ-4, examinees' abilities are often not accurately represented by the WASI Full Scale IQ-4. As such, it is necessary to take additional steps in the interpretive process.

## ≡ Rapid Reference 4.14

### Step 1: Interpret the Full Scale IQ

| Scale | IQ | Confidence Interval 90%/95% (circle one) | Percentile Rank | Descriptive Category |
|---|---|---|---|---|
| Verbal | 119 | 113–123 | 90 | High Average |
| Performance | 86 | 82–91 | 18 | Low Average |
| Full Scale IQ-4 | 102 | 99–105 | 55 | Average |

Note. If there is a significant difference between the Verbal IQ and the Performance IQ on the WASI, the Full Scale IQ should not be interpreted as a meaningful representation of the individual's overall performance.

If the two-subtest version of the WASI is administered, the FSIQ-2 should be reported. The FSIQ-2 is a fairly reliable score (average split-half for children and adults, respectively [$r = .93$, $r = .96$]; average test-retest for children and adults, respectively [$r = .85$, $r = .88$]). Since it is not possible to obtain a VIQ or PIQ for the two-subtest version of the WASI, the FSIQ-2 is the only score that is interpreted. On rare occasions, examiners may encounter extremely disparate Vocabulary and Matrix Reasoning T-Scores (e.g., 20 and 60). When the two T-scores are extremely disparate, examiners are cautioned against reporting the FSIQ-2. In these cases, an evaluation using a comprehensive intelligence test is warranted to provide more conclusive information regarding the examinee's verbal and nonverbal abilities. In addition to reporting the FSIQ-2, the examiner should indicate the confidence interval, percentile rank, and descriptive category. Once the FSIQ-2 score has been reported, the examiner has completed the interpretive process and does not proceed to Step 2.

## Step 2. Determine if the WASI Verbal-Performance IQ Discrepancy Is Statistically Significant

Like all Wechsler measures, the next level of global scores below the Full Scale IQ includes the Verbal IQ and the Performance IQ. The next step in WASI interpretation is to compute the size of the difference between the Verbal IQ and the Performance IQ. The direction of the discrepancy does not matter, but whether the difference is statistically significant is important.

The differences between WASI VIQ and PIQ scores required for statistical significance are presented in Table B.3 (p. 198) of the *WASI Manual*.

---

## ≡ *Rapid Reference 4.15*

### Step 2: Is the Verbal IQ Versus the Performance IQ Difference Significantly Different?

| | | | Significant | | Not | Is there a significant |
| VIQ | PIQ | Difference | ($p < .15$) | ($p < .05$) | Significant | difference? |
|-----|-----|------------|-------------|-------------|-------------|------------|
| 119 | 86 | 33 | 6 | 9 | 0–8 | Yes |

### Step 2 Decision Box

If the answer is no, there is not a significant difference between the VIQ and PIQ. → Explain the meaning of the scales not being significantly different. This concludes interpretation of the WASI for this individual. Do not proceed to Step 3.

If the answer is yes, there is a significant difference between the VIQ and PIQ. → Continue on to Step 3.

Note. James G. is a 32-year-old adult. Difference levels required for statistical difference for children ages 6–16 at the $p < .15$ and $p < .05$ levels are 8 and 11 respectively.

The critical values are provided for the .15 and .05 levels of significance for the 23 age groups and for the overall child and adult samples. Examiners must decide which level of confidence to use; for most testing purposes, the 85 percent level contains too much built-in error and it is recommended that a more conservative confidence level of 95 percent be used. A more conservative confidence level increases the likelihood that the difference is "true" and not due to chance.

If a significant Verbal IQ versus Performance IQ discrepancy is not found, then you may assume that the examinee's overall verbal and nonverbal skills are evenly developed and additional steps of WASI interpretation are unnecessary. If the difference score is equal to or larger than the critical value, it is statistically significant at that particular level of confidence. If there is a significant difference between the VIQ and PIQ in either direction (VIQ > PIQ or PIQ > VIQ), the Full Scale IQ-4 is not the best estimate of the child's or adult's cognitive functioning and should not be interpreted as a meaningful representation of the individual's overall performance. If a significant difference is found, move to the next step of interpretation to assess whether the difference between the VIQ and PIQ is *meaningful*.

### Step 3. Are the Verbal IQ and Performance IQ Differences Abnormally Large?

In Step 2, we determined whether the difference between Verbal and Performance IQs was large enough to be clinically significant. However, the level of significance of a difference does not tell us how frequently a discrepancy occurs in the normal population. In order for a discrepancy to be *meaningful*, it must occur in a relatively small percentage of individuals. In this next step, we determine whether the differences are rare or abnormal in the general population.

Most people have some sort of

> **DON'T FORGET**
> ....................................................
> In order for a Verbal IQ–Performance IQ difference to be *meaningful*, it must occur in a relatively small percentage of individuals.

discrepancy between their Verbal and Performance abilities. In the WASI standardization sample, about 50 percent of the adult sample obtained VIQ and PIQ score differences of 8 to 9 points, with 25 percent obtaining VIQ > PIQ differences and 25 percent obtaining PIQ > VIQ differences. However, just because an individual has scored significantly higher or lower on one of the IQs does not mean that his or her abilities are rare or abnormal. Furthermore, there is not information to indicate that there are problems with cognitive functioning.

How frequently a discrepancy occurs in the normal population is presented in Table B.4 (p. 199) of the *WASI Manual*. The data provided in Rapid Reference 4.16 shows the values needed for abnormality for the

## ≡ *Rapid Reference 4.16*

### Step 3: Are the Verbal IQ versus the Performance IQ Differences Abnormally Large?

| V-IQ vs. P-IQ Difference | Size of Difference Needed of Abnormality | | Does size meet abnormality criteria? |
|---|---|---|---|
| | **(VIQ > PIQ)** | **(PIQ > VIQ)** | |
| 33 | 14[a] | 13[a] | Yes |

### Step 3 Decision Box

| | | |
|---|---|---|
| If an *abnormal* difference is found | → then this *abnormally* large discrepancy should be interpreted. | → Explain the *abnormally* large Verbal and Performance differences. |
| If *no abnormal* differences are found | → then you must determine if noted differences are interpretable. | → Explain the noted differences. |

[a]Exact point values according to ability level are available in *WASI Manual* (Psychological Corporation, 1999; pp. 199).

> **DON'T FORGET**
> ..................................................
> Subtest strengths and weaknesses should not be interpreted when using the WASI.

Verbal IQ versus the Performance IQ discrepancy. The extreme 15 percent of the normal population (corresponding to approximately one standard deviation above the mean) is considered "abnormal" for our purposes. If an abnormally large difference exists, it should be interpreted. If an abnormally large VIQ-PIQ difference occurs, clinicians are provided with the information needed to determine an individual's areas of strengths and weaknesses and provide recommendations. If the difference is significant, but not abnormally large, this should be explained in the report. For example, one might state that, "The difference in verbal and nonverbal abilities was significant; however, this difference occurs in 25 percent of the adult population and is not clinically meaningful."

NOTE: Subtest strengths and weaknesses should not be interpreted when using the WASI. Interpretation of individual subtests is problematic because subtest scores are not as reliable as the FSIQ, VIQ, and PIQ. Furthermore, an attempt to make statements regarding an individual's cognitive processes based only on a brief sampling of his or her abilities would be imprudent.

## STRENGTHS AND WEAKNESSES OF THE TEST

There have been several published reports denoting the WASI's strengths and weaknesses since its publication in 1999 (Axelrod, 2002; Hays, Reas, & Shaw, 2002; Meyer, 2001; Ryan & Brown, 2005; Ryan, Carruthers, Miller, Souheaver, Gontkovsky, & Zehr, 2003; Stano, 2004). In this next section, we highlight what we feel are the major strengths and weaknesses of this measure in the areas of test development, administration and scoring, reliability and validity, standardization, and interpretation. We choose the Rapid Reference format to present this information most efficiently.

## Strengths and Weaknesses of the WASI

### Strengths

- Selection of subtests took into account specific cognitive functions of each subtest so that the widest variety of skills would be represented.

- Extensive effort was taken to develop parallel items of the WISC-III and WAIS-III subtests.

- T-scores have a far wider range of score points than scaled scores and can better differentiate ability levels.

- Inclusion of Matrix Reasoning subtest provides examinees with opportunity to demonstrate nonverbal abilities without time restrictions.

- WASI can be used across a wide range of ages (6–89).

- WASI normative IQs range from 50 to 160 and scores reflect high ceiling for children and low floor for adolescents and adults.

- For examinees who have experience with other Wechsler instruments, the WASI subtests are familiar and easy to use.

- Artwork in the WASI is colorful and appealing.

- Split-half reliability coefficients were excellent for the Verbal IQ, Performance IQ, Full Scale IQ-4, and Full Scale IQ-2 for both adults and children.

### Weaknesses

- There is not a theoretical explanation in the WASI Manual to provide rationale for using lower starting and stop items for individuals 45 to 89 on the Matrix Reasoning subtest.

- Stop points for younger examinees on Vocabulary and Similarities subtests may underestimate abilities of a small percentage of higher-functioning individuals. Similarly, stop points on Matrix Reasoning subtest for younger and older examinees may underestimate abilities.

- Test-retest stability is not excellent for the Matrix Reasoning subtest (average stability coefficients were .77 for the children's sample and .79 for the adult sample).

- Due to statistical concerns regarding a small number of variables, an exploratory factor analysis using standardization data is not available.

- Different types of items on the same subtest complicate interpretation. For example, items 1 through 4 on the Vocabulary and Similarities subtests are pictures while the remaining items on these subtests are verbal items.

*(continued)*

- For the four WASI subtests, split-half reliabilities are excellent across the 23 age groups. For the children's sample, reliability values ranged from .81 to .93 on verbal subtests and from .84 to .96 on performance subtests. For the adult sample, reliability values ranged from .84 to .98 on the verbal subtests and from .88 to .96 on the performance subtests.

- WASI subtest correlations with WISC-III and WAIS-III subtests are statistically significant and allow for the prediction of IQ confidence intervals.

- The WASI was well stratified and closely matches 1997 U.S. Census data.

- Care was taken to ensure that examiners were qualified to collect standardization data. Quality assurance measures were taken to assure accuracy of scoring and data entry.

- The WASI is linked to the WISC-III and the WAIS-III and provides tables for estimating IQ ranges on these measures.

- Tables are provided in the WASI Manual to indicate VIQ and PIQ differences required for significance when the four-subtest version is administered. Frequencies of VIQ-PIQ differences based on ability are also provided.

- The WASI samples only limited areas of cognitive functioning and does not include subtests from the third and fourth factors (e.g., Working Memory and Processing Speed) of the Wechsler full batteries.

- When the two-subtest version of the WASI is administered, it is not possible to obtain a Verbal or Performance IQ.

- The validity of Block Design as a measure of intelligence is problematic for examinees with fine or gross motor difficulties, and consequently an alternative brief IQ test is needed for these examinees.

- Because the Block Design and Matrix Reasoning subtests are highly dependent on visual-perceptual abilities, this measure is not appropriate for individuals with significant visual impairments.

## CLINICAL APPLICATIONS OF THE TEST

To determine the clinical sensitivity and utility of the four-subtest version of the WASI, independent data were collected with clinical populations including individuals with Mental Retardation and/or Down syndrome, giftedness, learning disabilities in reading and math, and traumatic brain injury, and are reported in the *WASI Manual* (Psychological Corporation, 1999, pp. 146–52). It is important to note that many of the sample sizes were relatively small in these studies and samples were selected by convenience. The purpose of these studies was to determine whether the WASI may provide a valid estimate of intellectual functioning for individuals in various groups. Findings suggest that although the WASI had adequate sensitivity for the screening of Mental Retardation, it does not have sufficient specificity for distinguishing the degree of Mental Retardation. Results suggested that the WASI may serve as an adequate brief instrument for screening individuals who are cognitively gifted. Previous research has suggested that individuals with reading disabilities tend to obtain relatively lower VIQs while individuals with math disabilities tend to obtain relatively lower PIQs (Rourke, 1998). For both reading and math disability groups, there was a trend toward relatively lower WASI scores consistent with previous research (Rourke, 1998); however, results were not significant. Interestingly, for a group with comorbid math and reading disabilities, the mean VIQ was significantly lower than the PIQ. In assessing individuals with traumatic brain injury, results are consistent with previous findings suggesting that individuals with moderate traumatic brain injury have some deficits in general cognitive functioning. While results of these small studies are positive, it is necessary for examiners to use a comprehensive intelligence measure (including Working Memory and Processing Speed factors) for diagnosing clinical populations.

## ~ TEST YOURSELF ~

1. **If an examinee provides a 2- or 1-point response to a Vocabulary subtest item but also includes a spoiled response, the examiner should score the best response.** True or False?

2. **The following are administration rules for the Block Design subtest except:**

   (a) For a 4-block design, only one block should have a red-and-white side facing up

   (b) Begin timing after the last word of instructions

   (c) Rotation of a design by 90 degrees is considered a failure

   (d) Do not permit the examinee to rotate the stimulus booklet

3. **If an examinee has not met the discontinue criterion on the Similarities subtest, the examiner should discontinue *after* the stop item specified for the examinee's age group.** True or False?

4. **If 30 seconds have elapsed on a Matrix Reasoning item and the examinee is clearly about to provide a response, the examiner should let the examinee respond and give credit if the response is correct.** True or False?

5 **According to the *WASI Manual* (Psychological Corporation, 1999), raw scores are converted to *T*-scores instead of scaled scores for the following reason:**

   (a) *T*-scores have a wider range of score points than scaled scores

   (b) *T*-scores have a narrower range of score points than scaled scores

   (c) *T*-scores have a range of 0–100 on the WASI

   (d) None of the above

6. **The moderate correlations found between the WASI and the WISC-IV, WAIS-III, and the WIAT provide support for**

   (a) reliability for the test.

   (b) validity for the test.

7. **Sarah, age 10, is administered the four-subtest version of the WASI and obtained a raw score of zero on the Vocabulary subtest. You should**

   (a) calculate the FSIQ-2 only.

   (b) calculate neither the VIQ nor the FSIQ-4.

   (c) calculate the VIQ, PIQ, and FSIQ-4.

   (d) consider the entire test invalid.

8. **Stop points for younger examinees on the Vocabulary and Similarities subtests may have implications for testing what population?**

    (a) Mentally retarded children

    (b) Children with traumatic brain injury

    (c) Children with Attention-Deficit/Hyperactivity Disorder

    (d) Gifted children

9. **You have analyzed Shane's test results on the two-subtest version of the WASI and there is a 40-point difference between his Vocabulary and Matrix Reasoning T-scores. You should**

    (a) interpret the FSIQ-2.

    (b) indicate that the FSIQ-2 is not the best indicator of intelligence and recommend that a comprehensive intelligence measure be administered.

    (c) throw out the entire assessment.

    (d) administer the Similarities and Block Design subtests and interpret the FSIQ-4.

10. **It is possible for a WASI Verbal-Performance IQ difference to be statistically significant without the difference being abnormally large.** True or False?

*Answers:* 1. False; 2. c; 3. True; 4. True; 5. a; 6. b; 7. b; 8. d; 9. b; 10. True

Five

# THE WIDE RANGE INTELLIGENCE
# TEST (WRIT)

The WRIT (Glutting, Adams, & Sheslow, 2000) is a four-subtest ability measure requiring approximately 30 minutes for administration. Scoring is objective and accomplished by the skilled examiner in about 5 minutes. The WRIT is touted by the authors as "a new direction for ability measures because it delivers a psychometrically sound product with great efficiency" (Glutting et al., 2000, p. 1). Originally published by Wide Range, Inc., the WRIT—as well as other Wide Range products—is now published by Psychological Assessment Resources, Inc. (PAR).

The WRIT is standardized on 2,285 individuals from 4 years through 85 years of age drawn to be representative of the United States population-at-large with stratification on the basis of age, gender, ethnicity, regional residence, and educational level, as determined from the 1997 U.S. Bureau of the Census data. The four WRIT subtests, entitled Verbal Analogies, Vocabulary, Matrices, and Diamonds, represent well-known tasks that have been researched widely in the field of aptitude testing for many decades. These subtests are described in Table 5.1. The WRIT is intended as an efficient measure of intelligence that can be used even in the diagnosis of cognitive disorders. We recommend it as a brief measure of intelligence that is particularly useful in screening of intellectual level, much as the WASI would be used, whenever an examinee has no fine or gross motor

Portions of this chapter are adapted with permission of the copyright holder, Psychological Assessment Resources, Inc., from Glutting et al. (2000), *Wide Range Intelligence Test,* Lutz, FL: PAR, Inc.

**Table 5.1  Subtest Names and Designations for the WRIT**

| | |
|---|---|
| | **Verbal Subtests** |
| Verbal Analogies | On this task, examinees are asked to complete a verbal analogy presented orally by the examiner (e.g., rocks are hard and cotton is _____). The task assesses verbal reasoning skills. |
| Vocabulary | On this task, examinees must define a word presented orally by the examiner (e.g., What is a rock?). This subtest assesses work knowledge and verbal learning, both incidental and purposive. |
| | **Visual Subtests** |
| Matrices | A traditional matrix analogies task, on this subtest examinees choose a picture from multiple alternatives that completes an implied pattern or relationship among pictures presented as the stimulus. This task assesses nonverbal reasoning, spatial ability, and visualization skills. |
| Diamonds | On this task, examinees are required to reproduce a pictured design using green and tan diamond-shaped chips. This task assesses fine motor skill, constructional praxis, and the ability to analyze and synthesize elements of a whole. |

problems affecting the upper extremities, and in other applications as detailed in Chapter 1 of this volume.

The WRIT subtests include two from the verbal domain and two from the visual domain, yielding a Verbal IQ, Visual IQ, and a General IQ, all scaled (as are the subtests) to a standard score metric with a mean of 100 and standard deviation of 15.

The choice of the term *visual* to designate the nonverbal or more traditionally viewed performance domain is ill explained and, we believe, unfortunate. The Visual IQ is intended on the WRIT as prin-

**DON'T FORGET**

All WRIT scores, including subtest scores and IQs, are scaled to the most common of IQ metrics, Mean = 100, SD = 15.

cipally a measure of fluid intelligence and the Verbal IQ as a measure of crystallized intelligence. Given the emphasis on interpreting the Verbal and Visual IQs as measures of crystallized and fluid intelligence, respectively, in the WRIT manual, use of these terms would have been more clarifying. (See Rapid References 5.1 and 5.2.)

In the process of developing the WRIT, the authors set out five key goals (also see Rapid Reference 5.2). They attempted to design an instrument that would be consistent with several of the major contemporary theories of intelligence now popular. The WRIT was designed to correlate highly with longer, traditional tests of intelligence. Data in the WRIT Manual (Glutting et al., 2000) emphasizes correlations with the WISC-III and WAIS-III. A set of tasks was chosen that would cover a wide age range so that children and adults would be assessed on a common test. The WRIT was designed to be user friendly with regard to administration, scoring, and interpretation. And, lastly, the authors wanted to create a test that would be "fun for the examinee" (Glutting et al., 2000, p. iii).

*≣ Rapid Reference 5.1*

### The Wide Range Intelligence Test (WRIT)

**Authors:** Joseph Glutting, Wayne Adams, & David Sheslow
**Publication Date(s):** 2000
**What the test measures:** Verbal, visual, and general intelligence
**Qualifications of examiner:** Qualified psychologists or other professionals who have completed formal coursework and supervision in individual assessment
**Publisher:** Psychological Assessment Resources, Inc. (PAR)
16204 N. Florida Avenue
Lutz, FL 33549
(800) 331-TEST (8378)
www.parinc.com
**Prices** (as of August 1, 2006): WRIT complete kit = $275.00

## ≡ *Rapid Reference 5.2*

### The Authors' Key Objectives in Developing the WRIT

In developing the WRIT, Glutting et al. (2000) set out to produce an intelligence test that would:

- show consistency with current theories of intelligence
- correlate highly with much longer measures of intelligence
- allow assessment on a common test of children and adults
- be user friendly (i.e., easy to learn, administer, score, and interpret)
- be fun for the examinee

## USER QUALIFICATIONS

The *WRIT Manual* admonishes that examiners administering the test should be either qualified psychologists or professionals from related disciplines who have completed formal coursework that includes supervision in individual intelligence testing (e.g., educational diagnosticians, some counselors). These requirements would appear to rule out administration and scoring of the WRIT by neuropsychological technicians and related extenders of psychological testing services. Glutting et al. (2000) also recommend that examiners have knowledge and skills related to lifespan development and the special problems associated with the evaluation of preschool children, adolescents, and

**DON'T FORGET**

User qualifications for the WRIT require formal coursework in individual testing along with supervised experience in the use of individually administered tests of ability.

**CAUTION**

Knowing how to administer and score the WRIT is not enough. Examiners must also be skilled with the specific age group to be assessed. Evaluation of preschoolers, adolescents, and senior adults requires different sets of knowledge and skills.

adults among other special groups due to the wide age range covered by the WRIT.

## STANDARDIZATION AND PSYCHOMETRIC PROPERTIES

A summary of the information presented in the WRIT manual regarding its standardization and psychometric properties follows. Greater detail on each topic is available in Glutting et al. (2000).

### Item Development

In most respects, one of the strengths of the WRIT is the level of documentation of its psychometric characteristics. The initial item development and tryout is a significant exception to this rubric. Chapter 9 of the *WRIT Manual* (Glutting et al., 2000), indicates that only twice as many items for each subtest as are on the published version were written that "were thought to be relevant to the variables being measured with the four subtests of the WRIT" (p. 133). A Rasch item analysis was performed as was a "more subjective review of issues related to item bias" (p. 133) in order to choose the final items. Once the items had been selected, a set of Rasch model comparisons of the item calibrations across multiple ethnic groups (e.g., Anglo/ African-American, Anglo/Hispanic, African-American/Hispanic) and across gender were calculated. The Rasch-derived item calibration indexes correlated .99 for every set of group comparisons, denoting that the item set taken as a whole functions in a highly similar manner across all groups evaluated.

## CAUTION

Some aspects of the psycho-metric details of the WRIT are exceptionally well explained and presented in detail in the *WRIT Manual*, but other psychometric characteristics are presented less fully. Always be familiar with the key descriptions of the WRIT's characteristics as detailed in the Manual.

## Standardization

The WRIT was normed on a sample of 2,285 persons drawn from the four regions of the United States as defined by the Bureau of the Census (Northeast, South, North Central, and West). Dates of data collection and specific states included are not indi-

### CAUTION

While the WRIT standardization sample closely matches the target population demographic characteristics for ages 4 years through 18 years, there are significant disparities in its match to the target population in the adult age ranges.

cated in the manual, however, the sampling plan was designed to match the 1997 U.S. Bureau of the Census demographic statistics on the basis of age, gender, ethnicity, educational attainment (for ages 4 through 18, parent educational level was employed), and region of residence. The obtained sample closely matches the Census Bureau data at some ages but not others. The closest match to the Census statistics was obtained for ages 4 years to 18 years. However, the adult sample statistics are often askew from the target population statistics, and examiners will need to be especially cautious in applications of the WRIT in the adult age range.

## Scaling

All subtests and IQs from the WRIT are scaled as standard scores with a mean of 100 and SD of 15. Percentiles are provides for each standard score. However, the method of derivation of the WRIT standard scores is not described or otherwise articulated in the WRIT manual (Glutting et al., 2000) beyond an indication on page two that "statistical distributions" were used to compute standard scores.

## Reliability of WRIT Scores

Internal consistency reliability estimates for the four WRIT subtests are quite high. As can be seen in Table 5.2 (based on the WRIT standard-

**Table 5.2 Standard Errors of Measurement (SEMs) and Internal Consistency Reliability Estimates (r) for WRIT Scores for Four Age Groups**

| | | General IQ | Verbal IQ | Visual IQ | Vocabulary | Verbal Analogies | Matrices | Diamonds |
|---|---|---|---|---|---|---|---|---|
| | | | | | | | | |
| Ages 4–5 years | r | .93 | .91 | .89 | .89 | .84 | .88 | .94 |
| N = 350 | SEM | 5.5 | 6.2 | 6.8 | 6.8 | 8.1 | 7.1 | 5.1 |
| Ages 6–12 years | r | .95 | .91 | .94 | .91 | .83 | .93 | .85 |
| N = 700 | SEM | 4.7 | 6.2 | 5.1 | 6.2 | 8.4 | 5.5 | 7.9 |
| Ages 13–18 years | r | .94 | .89 | .91 | .89 | .76 | .85 | .90 |
| N = 525 | SEM | 5.1 | 6.8 | 6.2 | 6.8 | 9.7 | 7.9 | 6.5 |
| Ages 19 & up | r | .97 | .96 | .94 | .93 | .83 | .92 | .91 |
| N = 710 | SEM | 3.6 | 4.2 | 5.1 | 5.5 | 8.4 | 5.9 | 6.2 |
| Mean | r | .95 | .94 | .92 | .91 | .84 | .90 | .93 |
| | SEM | 4.7 | 5.1 | 5.9 | 6.2 | 8.1 | 6.5 | 5.5 |

*Reliability Coefficient*

ization sample data) most of the coefficients are above .90 for the four age groups reported. Of the values reported in Table 5.2, only the reliability estimate for Verbal Analogies at ages 13 to 18 drops into the .70s (.76). Separate reli-

## DON'T FORGET

The WRIT IQs (General, Verbal, and Visual) have average internal consistency reliability estimates across age in the low to mid .90s.

ability data across gender and ethnicity are not reported. Stability coefficients are likewise strong, over an average 30-day period, with values consistently in the .90s for the three WRIT IQs and subtest level coefficients ranging from the .70s to .90s across age.

The internal consistency and test-retest, or stability, coefficients for the WRIT IQs appear to be more than sufficient for virtually all purposes for which brief IQ tests may be deemed appropriate. The WRIT IQs yield mean standard errors of measurement of 4.7 for the General IQ, 5.1 for the Verbal IQ, and 5.9 for the Visual IQ. Some variability is noted across age with changes of more than 50 percent in the value of the standard error of measurement seen for each IQ across age (see Table 5.2). All remain clearly acceptable for most purposes. Overall, reliability data for the WRIT suggest the WRIT IQs are appropriately reliable to serve as either first or second screening gates and that the WRIT may be used for other brief intelligence testing purposes described throughout this volume. In fact, the internal consistency and stability of WRIT IQs are comparable to those of intelligence tests of far greater length.

### Validity of WRIT Score Interpretation

Two types of validity evidence for WRIT score interpretation are emphasized in the WRIT manual: internal evidence (primarily a series of various forms of factor analysis) and correlation with other measures of intelligence and achievement. Factor analyses are reported for the entire sample as well as separately by gender, ethnicity, educational level, and age level.

Table 5.3 presents estimates of the degree to which each WRIT sub-

**Table 5.3 Estimates of g-loading of WRIT Subtests and Two-Factor Promax Pattern Loadings for the WRIT Standardization Sample**

| Subtest | Estimated g-loading | Promax Loadings | |
|---|---|---|---|
| | | Factor 1 | Factor 2 |
| Vocabulary | .80 | .81 | −.04 |
| Verbal Analogies | .82 | .68 | .12 |
| Diamonds | .64 | −.02 | .59 |
| Matrices | .72 | .19 | .44 |

test assesses *g,* or general intelligence. These estimates are taken from the first, unrotated factor resulting from a principal components factor analysis. All four of these loadings are considered to be relatively high, indicating measurement of a common dimension that, based upon the item content of the WRIT subtests, is strongly associated with general intelligence. Results of a two-factor Promax rotation (of two factors forced from a principal components analysis) are shown in Table 5.3 as well. The pattern and magnitude of these coefficients strongly supports the division of the four WRIT subtests into two dimensions that, while strong measures of *g,* measure some significant subordinate aspects of intelligence as well. Based on the test content, these subdomains do appear to be closely aligned with crystallized (Verbal IQ) and fluid (Visual IQ) abilities.

The *WRIT Manual* also presents correlational studies between the WRIT IQs and the WISC-III and WAIS-III. These results are summarized in Table 5.4. These correlations are not corrected for the large standard deviations present in the score distributions in both studies. The SDs of the IQs ranged from 16.0 to 22.4 across the two studies. Such large SDs can result in spuriously high correlations and, when both variables of a cor-

**DON'T FORGET**
.....................................
Estimates of g-loadings for the WRIT subtests are relatively high, ranging from .64 for Matrices to .81 for Verbal Analogies.

## Table 5.4  Correlations (Uncorrected) Between WRIT Scores and WISC-III and WAIS-III Scores

| | WRIT Score | | |
| | General IQ | Verbal IQ | Visual IQ |
|---|---|---|---|
| WISC-III | | | |
|   Full Scale IQ | .90 | .85 | .80 |
|   Verbal IQ | .88 | .85 | .76 |
|   Performance IQ | .85 | .78 | .78 |
| WAIS-III | | | |
|   Full Scale IQ | .91 | .89 | .85 |
|   Verbal IQ | .88 | .90 | .80 |
|   Performance IQ | .86 | .80 | .85 |

*Note.* $N = 100$.

relation have inflated SDs as occurs here, correction formulas may not produce accurate results. So, while the relationships presented in Table 5.4 are extremely high, the true values are almost certainly lower. They would not be so low as to call the overall association or its pattern into question, however. Even the most conservative corrections would still indicate substantial correlations between each WRIT IQ and each Wechsler IQ. The pattern and magnitude of the values in Table 5.4 are strongly supportive of the interpretation of the three WRIT IQs as measures of general intelligence. Little support is seen here for the differentiation of the Verbal and Visual IQs into separate domains.

However, the WRIT manual also reports correlations between the WRIT IQs and Reading, Spelling, and Arithmetic scores on the Wide Range Achievement Test–Third Edition (WRAT-3; Wilkinson, 1993). These correlations are reported for four separate age groups. For Reading and Spelling, the Verbal IQ has a higher correlation (but only somewhat so) than the Visual IQ at all four age levels. Results are essentially equivocal across the Verbal and Visual IQs for the prediction of Arithmetic scores on the WRAT-3. Overall, the WRIT IQs show correlations with WRAT-3 scores in the range of .36 to .58 at age 5 years, .36 to .51 for ages

# DON'T FORGET

Factor analytic evidence strongly supports the structure of the WRIT across age, gender, ethnicity, and educational level.

6 to 12 years, .48 to .64 for ages 13 to 18 years, and .38 to .60 for ages 19 and older.

No studies are reported for various samples of clinical groups on the WRIT.

Overall, validity evidence presented in the WRIT manual strongly supports its use as a measure of general intelligence. The division of the four subtests into Verbal IQ and Visual IQ scales receives less support. While the factor-analytic evidence is good for this division, the criterion-related evidence shows very little divergence in the pattern of correlations. However, the evidence is more than sufficient to recommend the WRIT for the various purposes for which we see brief intelligence tests as appropriate per our discussions in Chapter 1 of this work.

## ADMINISTERING AND SCORING THE WRIT

The WRIT subtests are administered in the following order: Matrices, Verbal Analogies, Diamonds, and Vocabulary. The length of instructions varies substantially from one subtest to another, as does the level of detail regarding administration on the WRIT record form. In some cases (e.g., Diamonds), instructions are contained in the picture booklet while for others (e.g., Vocabulary) most essential instructions appear on the record form. The test is nevertheless easy to learn and easy to administer and score provided one meets the stated user qualifications and engages in a few practice administrations.

All of the WRIT subtests have age-designated starting points accompanied by specific basal and ceiling rules. Whenever an examinee fails to reach a basal when beginning at the age-designated starting point, items on the WRIT are not administered in reverse order as is commonplace on many intelligence tests. Rather, when a basal is not obtained at the starting point, the examiner returns to the next earlier age-designated starting point and proceeds according to directions for this younger starting point, falling back again as needed.

A stopwatch is recommended for accurate administration of the Matrices and the Diamonds subtests.

**DON'T FORGET**

A stopwatch is recommended for accurate administration of the Matrices and the Diamonds subtests.

Overall, scoring is reasonably objective despite the presence of a 0,1,2 scoring rubric on the Vocabulary subtest that requires fine judgments at times. The *WRIT Manual* reports an interscorer reliability coefficient of .98 across 40 cases scored independently by two examiners.

General guidelines for administration and scoring of each subtest are reviewed in the following.

**Subtest 1: Matrices**

Materials: Record Form, Manual, Easel Book, stopwatch
Time Limit: 30 seconds for items 1–35
45 seconds for items 36–44

### Description

A traditional matrix or nonverbal analogies task, the Matrices subtest measures nonverbal reasoning abilities with at times an emphasis on visual-spatialization skills. The examinee is asked to choose from among multiple options on a picture that complete a puzzle, theme, spatial relationship, or a concept.

### Begin Rule

Age-based starting points are specified on the Record Form.

### Basal Level

A basal level consists of two consecutive correct responses. When

**DON'T FORGET**

Matrices has time limits. Items 1 through 35 allow 30 seconds. Items 36 through 44 allow 45 seconds.

a basal level cannot be obtained, the subtest may still be given, but the derived score may overestimate the examinee's ability level. If the examinee does not provide correct responses on the first two items, the Reverse Rule is applied.

### Reverse Rule

If the examinee fails to obtain a basal level on the first two test items, stop and go back to the next age-designated starting point and administer two items. If a basal is then obtained, continue testing until the Discontinue Rule is met. If a basal level is not obtained, go back to the next age-designated starting point and repeat this procedure until a basal is obtained or you reach item 1.

### Discontinue Rule

Stop administering Matrices when the examinee fails (earns a raw score of 0) on 4 out of 5 consecutively administered items, unless a basal level has not yet been reached. If a basal has not been reached, continue to go back as detailed previously. Once a basal has been established, the test is discontinued at the first point where the Discontinue Rule would apply if the items had been administered in numerical order.

### General Information

This subtest is timed. Allow 30 seconds for a response to items 1 through 35 and 45 seconds for items 36 through 44. Timing begins as soon as the directions are given and the examiner has displayed properly the appropriate picture book page. Five seconds before time expires on the item, if no answer has been given, prompt the examinee by saying, "Guess, because it is time to try another one."

> **DON'T FORGET**
>
> On Matrices, 5 seconds before time expires, prompt the examinee by saying, "Guess, because it is time to try another one."

### Scoring

Matrices items are scored one point for each correct response for items 1 through 35 and two points for items 36 through 44. Correct responses are indicated via a numbering system on the Record Form.

## Subtest 2: Verbal Analogies

Materials: Record Form, Manual
Time Limit: None

### Description
Verbal Analogies assesses verbal reasoning skills in combination with word knowledge, requiring the examinee to deduce various verbal relationships. It is one of the oldest, most researched, and common of verbal reasoning tasks, appearing in similar form on many other ability tests. There is no time limit. Items are presented as incomplete sentences, read in a steady but conversational form. Items may be repeated only if the examinee requests repetition or clearly misperceives the examiner's pronunciation. No guidance is given on the number of repetitions permitted. Instructions are otherwise simple, clear, and straightforward for the examiner and the examinee.

### Begin Rule
Age-based starting points are specified on the Record Form

### Basal Level
A basal level consists of two consecutive correct responses. When a basal level cannot be obtained, the subtest may still be given, but the derived score may overestimate the examinee's ability level. If the examinee does not provide correct responses on the first two items, the Reverse Rule is applied.

### Reverse Rule
If the examinee fails to obtain a basal level on the first two test items, stop and go back to the next age-designated starting point and adminis-

ter two items. If a basal is then obtained, continue testing until the Discontinue Rule is met. If a basal level is not obtained, go back to the next age-designated starting point and repeat this procedure until a basal is obtained or you reach item 1.

### Discontinue Rule

Stop administering Verbal Analogies when the examinee fails (earns a raw score of 0) on 5 consecutively administered items, unless a basal level has not yet been reached. If a basal has not been reached, continue to go back as detailed previously. Once a basal has been established, the test is discontinued at the first point where the Discontinue Rule would apply if the items had been administered in numerical order.

### Scoring

Verbal Analogies items are scored pass-fail (1,0) for all items (1–36). Correct responses are *not* listed on the examiner record form, but appear on page 19 of the WRIT manual (Glutting et al., 2000). Most items have only one acceptable response; however, some items do have alternative correct responses listed.

## Subtest 3: Diamonds

Materials: Box containing diamond-shaped puzzle pieces, Manual, picture book, stopwatch, Record Form

Time Limit: Time limits for the Diamonds items vary from 15 seconds for items 1–2, 30 seconds for items 3–11, 60 seconds for item 12, and 90 seconds for items 13–14

### DON'T FORGET

Diamonds is the most difficult of the WRIT subtests to administer accurately and will require the most practice.

### Description

The WRIT Diamonds subtest is a measure of nonverbal ability requiring the examinee to analyze a picture of a design and then synthesize or create the design from a set of two-color puzzle pieces (called chips), all of which are in some form of a diamond shape. The examiner presents the pictures of the constructed puzzle or shape to the examinee, who is given a set of randomly arranged puzzle pieces or chips from which to construct a design that matches the picture. On items 1 through 3, two trials are allowed. On the remaining items, only one try is given. On the last five items, an examinee can receive variable bonus points for rapid completion of the pictured design.

> **DON'T FORGET**
> ........................................................
> Time limits on the Diamonds subtest items range from 15 seconds on the first two items to 90 seconds for the last two items.

### Begin Rule

Age-based starting points are specified on the Record Form.

### Basal Level

A basal level consists of two consecutive correct responses. When a basal level cannot be obtained, the subtest may still be given, but the derived score may overestimate the examinee's ability level. If the examinee does not provide correct responses on the first two items, the Reverse Rule is applied.

### Reverse Rule

If the examinee fails to obtain a basal level on the first two test items, stop and go back to the next age-designated starting point and administer two items. If a basal is then obtained, continue testing until the Discontinue Rule is met. If a basal level is not obtained, go back to the next age-designated starting point and repeat this procedure until a basal is obtained or you reach item 1.

### Discontinue Rule

Stop administering Diamonds subtest when the examinee fails (earns a raw score of 0) on 2 consecutively administered items, unless a basal level has not yet been reached. If a basal has not been reached, continue to go

# DON'T FORGET

Rotations of 30° or less from horizontal is acceptable for all items on Diamonds but rotations that exceed 30° are corrected by the examiner but scored as a failure, except for the first rotation, which is corrected but given full credit.

back as detailed previously. Once a basal has been established, the test is discontinued at the first point where the Discontinue Rule would apply if the items had been administered in numerical order.

## Scoring

Diamonds items can earn variable scores depending upon whether completed in a single or in multiple trials and bonus points can be earned on the last five items for quick performance. If an examinee rotates a response up to 30° from horizontal, this is considered acceptable if the design is otherwise correct. If a rotation of more than 30° occurs, the examiner corrects the rotation every time it occurs. However, credit is given only for the first rotation of more than 30°; all subsequent rotations exceeding 30° are scored as a failure.

## Subtest 4: Vocabulary

Materials: Record Form, Manual
Time Limit: None

### Description

The WRIT Vocabulary is a traditional oral test of word definition. The examiner presents a word orally and the examinee defines it (except for the first few items for the youngest of examinees who can respond by pointing to named body parts on the first two items). The first five items are scored as pass-fail (1,0) and items 6 through 33 are scored according to the quality of the response as 2, 1, or 0.

Items for Vocabulary may be repeated if requested by the examinee or if the examinee obviously misperceived the examiner's pronunciation. Examiners are also mandated to query an examinee for elaboration of ambiguous or vague responses that can not be classified clearly into a 0-,

1-, or 2-point response category. No overarching or clear conceptual guide is given to classification of responses in general. Each item has specific criteria that will need to be followed by the examiner.

### Begin Rule
Age-based starting points are specified on the Record Form.

### Basal Level
A basal level consists of two consecutive correct responses. When a basal level cannot be obtained, the subtest may still be given, but the derived score may overestimate the examinee's ability level. If the examinee does not provide correct responses on the first two items, the Reverse Rule is applied.

### Reverse Rule
If the examinee fails to obtain a basal level on the first two test items, stop and go back to the next age-designated starting point and administer two items. If a basal is then obtained, continue testing until the Discontinue Rule is met. If a basal level is not obtained, go back to the next age-designated starting point and repeat this procedure until a basal is obtained or you reach item 1.

### Discontinue Rule
Stop administering Vocabulary subtest when the examinee fails (earns a raw score of 0) on 4 consecutively administered items, unless a basal level has not yet been reached. If a basal has not been reached, continue to go back as detailed previously. Once a basal has been established, the test is discontinued at the first point where the Discontinue Rule would apply if the items had been administered in numerical order.

### Scoring
The Manual provides a detailed scoring guide for Vocabulary on pages 29 through 45. Each item has its own criteria, with few generalities applying. The only general scoring rules are that "the exact wording found in standard dictionaries" (p. 29) are given full credit. Interestingly, and potentially to the disadvantage of some groups, slang and regional usages

**DON'T FORGET**
........................................................

Use the sum of the standard scores for all four WRIT subtests to look up the General IQ in the IQ tables beginning on page 173 of the *WRIT Manual*.

that do not appear in standard dictionaries are not scored beyond 0. When more than one answer is proffered by an examinee, unless all fall into the same scoring category, the examinee is required to select a best answer. Items 1 through 5 are scored 0 or 1 and all remaining items are scored 0, 1, or 2, according to the detailed criteria presented in the scoring guide.

## Obtaining Standard Scores

Raw scores for each subtest are converted to standard scores with a mean of 100 and SD of 15 using tables in the *WRIT Manual* (Glutting et al., 2000). The sum of the standard scores for Verbal Analogies and Vocabulary is then used to look up the Verbal IQ. The sum of the standard scores for Matrices and Diamonds is used to locate the Visual IQ. The sum of the standard scores for all four subtests is used to locate the General IQ. (See Rapid Reference 5.3.)

## INTERPRETATION

Although the *WRIT Manual* (Glutting et al., 2000) provides information for subtest-level score interpretations, we do not recommend this level of analysis for reasons consistent with the conclusions of Reynolds and Kamphaus (2003b, see especially Chapter 1). The three WRIT IQs are the recommended metrics for interpretation of WRIT performance. All of the WRIT IQs are scaled to the familiar IQ metric of a mean of 100 and SD of 15. Table 5.5 provides qualitative descriptions of various levels of performance on the WRIT when expressed as standard scores. These descriptive labels are the ones recommended by the WRIT authors.

Interpretation should begin by providing the standard scores and

**Table 5.5 Recommended Qualitative Descriptions of Various WRIT Standard Score Levels**

| IQ Range | Descriptive Label |
|----------|-------------------|
| 130 and above | Very Superior |
| 120–129 | Superior |
| 111–119 | High Average |
| 90–110 | Average |
| 80–89 | Low Average |
| 70–79 | Borderline |
| 69 and below | Very Low |

*Source.* Glutting et al. (2000).

accompanying percentile ranks and qualitative description. The General IQ is a strong measure of *g* and should be interpreted as such. The Verbal and Visual IQs of the WRIT are interpreted best as measures of crystallized and fluid intelligence, respectively, for most examinees. Differences of about 14 points between the WRIT Verbal and Visual IQs denotes a significant difference between these two scores (see Table 6.3, p. 68 of Glutting et al., 2000, for exact values by age). When such a difference is present, it indicates higher levels of performance, and, by inference, superior ability in one domain versus the other. However, 14-point discrepancies are relatively common, occurring in about 30 percent of the population. It is not until reaching a difference of 24 points that the frequency of occurrence drops to 10 percent and a difference 29 points to get to 5 percent.

When used as a screening measure, the presence of a significant difference between the Verbal and Visual IQs should prompt additional assessment, depending upon the reason for the initial evaluation. When no significant difference occurs between these IQs, the General IQ becomes the primary score for interpretation and can be used much as any summary IQ would be used in a screening setting and as delineated more fully in Chapter 1 of this work.

## ≡ Rapid Reference 5.3

### Strengths and Weaknesses of the WRIT

| Strengths | Weaknesses |
|---|---|

**Strengths**

- Familiar, time-tested tasks chosen for inclusion.
- Artwork is colorful and appealing.
- Assesses verbal and nonverbal dimensions.
- A wide range of IQs is available at most ages beginning at age 7 years (35 to 155 at most ages from 7 years to 84 years).
- Sample statistics are a very close match to target population demographic characteristics at ages 4 years to 18 years.
- IQs have reliabilities above .90 across age.
- Factor analyses strongly support the General, Visual, and Verbal IQ structure of the WRIT across age, gender, ethnicity, and educational level.
- Very high correlations with comprehensive measures of intelligence.
- Test bias studies were conducted at the scale level.

**Weaknesses**

- Very limited information on item development and selection provided.
- Only conducted subjective reviews of gender and ethnic bias at the item level with no statistical tests for item bias.
- Sample statistics are a poor match to target population demographic characteristics within the adult age range.
- Diamonds subtest not appropriate for use with examinees with gross or fine motor impairments of the upper extremities.
- Sample items are not provided.

## 🐟  TEST YOURSELF  🐟

1. **The WRIT contains 4 subtests that measure primarily _____ and _____.**

   (a) general knowledge and recall

   (b) crystallized intelligence and fluid intelligence

   (c) verbal reasoning and spatial ability

   (d) language development and constructional praxis

   (e) verbal memory and visual-motor integration skills

2. **WRIT subtests are scaled to a mean of _____ and SD of _____.**

   (a) 10, 3

   (b) 0, 1

   (c) 50, 10

   (d) 100, 15

   (e) 5, 2

3. **The WRIT IQs are scaled to a mean of _____ and SD of _____.**

   (a) 10, 3

   (b) 0, 1

   (c) 50, 10

   (d) 100, 15

   (e) 5, 2

4. **Since it is a brief intelligence test, no formal or academic training is required to administer and score the WRIT.** True or False?

5. **The most difficult WRIT subtest to learn to administer accurately is**

   _____.

   (a) Vocabulary

   (b) Verbal Analogies

   (c) Matrices

   (d) Diamonds

   *(continued)*

6. Rotations of _____ or less are acceptable for credit when scoring items for the Diamonds subtest.

   (a) 10°

   (b) 20°

   (c) 30°

   (d) 45°

   (e) 90°

7. The mean internal consistency reliability coefficient for each of the WRIT subtests is best described as being _____.

   (a) .60 or higher

   (b) .70 or higher

   (c) .80 or higher

   (d) .90 or higher

   (e) .93 or higher

8. The WRIT subtest with the lowest g-loading (.64) is _____.

   (a) Vocabulary

   (b) Verbal Analogies

   (c) Matrices

   (d) Diamonds

9. According to the WRIT Manual, the correlation between the WRIT General IQ and Full Scale IQs for both WISC-III and WAIS-III are approximately _____.

   (a) .60

   (b) .70

   (c) .80

   (d) .90

   (e) .96

10. Across age, a difference of 14 points between the **WRIT** Verbal and Visual IQs is statistically significant at $p \leq .05$. This difference occurs in about _____ of the **WRIT** standardization sample.

(a) 1%

(b) 5%

(c) 25%

(d) 30%

(e) 50%

*Answers:* 1. b; 2. d; 3. d; 4. False; 5. d; 6. c; 7. c; 8. d; 9. d; 10. d

# Six

# SAMPLE EVALUATIONS USING BRIEF INTELLIGENCE TESTS

This chapter presents examples of brief evaluations using the KBIT-2, RIST, WASI, and WRIT. The purpose of providing sample case reports is to illustrate specific examples of the use of brief intelligence measures incorporating principles of administration, scoring, and interpretation. Reports include the following: identifying information about the child, reason for referral, background and history, behavioral observations during the assessment, test results and interpretation, summary and conclusions, and recommendations. For all cases presented within this chapter, test scores are presented prior to the report.

## DON'T FORGET

### Information to Include in the Identifying Information Section of a Report

- Examinee's name
- Date of birth
- Age
- Grade in school (if applicable)
- Date of testing
- Date of report
- Examiner's name and title

# DON'T FORGET

## Information to Include in Reason for Referral Section

- List name and position of referral source
- Reason the individual is to be evaluated—What questions are to be addressed?
- Concerns of parent, caregiver, teacher, or examinee (if applicable)
- Previous diagnoses, disabilities, or medical concerns

# DON'T FORGET

## Information to Include in Background Information Section

Provide pertinent information that has been obtained from all sources, including the referral source, family members, examinee, teachers, medical records, and so on. Do not include needless details or gossip. Following are examples of information that should be included:

- Current family dynamics (spouse, children, siblings, etc.)
- Medical and psychiatric history
- Developmental history
- Educational history (note any special services)
- Employment history (for adults)
- Previous therapeutic intervention
- Current stressors
- Summary of past evaluations

When writing reports, however, test scores most often are included either within the test results and interpretation section or at the very end of the report in a section labeled "Psychometric Summary," although many formats and styles are acceptable.

# DON'T FORGET

## Information to Include in Behavioral Observations Section

- Note significant patterns of performance that occurred during testing
- Sequence information in order of importance
- Provide specific examples of examinee's behavior

Following are examples of information that may be included:

### Appearance

- Size: height and weight
- Facial characteristics
- Grooming and cleanliness
- Clothing style
- Does the person look his or her chronological age?

### Behavior

- Level of eye contact
- Does he or she initiate conversation or merely answer examiner's questions?
- Speech articulation and language patterns
- Attention span/distractibility (Does he or she ask for items to be repeated?)
- Activity level (excessive talking, standing, foot wiggling, etc.)
- Level of cooperativeness
- Motivation to do well
- How does the examinee go about solving problems?
- How does the examinee react to failure or difficult tasks?
- Examinee's need for approval and response to positive praise

### Validity of Test Results

- Statements such as, "Results of this assessment are considered a valid reflection of Mark's current level of functioning."
- If results are felt to be invalid, explain why.

# DON'T FORGET

### Information to Include in Test Results and Interpretation Section

- Provide information in paragraph form.
- Provide full name of test administered and what it measures.
- Provide IQs, Index scores, and percentile ranks when describing the examinee's scores. When discussing performance on subtests, provide scaled scores and percentile ranks. Do not include raw scores. Provide your reader with descriptive ranges to assist with interpretation.
- Describe the abilities that are tapped with each subtest. The reader has no idea what "Guess What" measures.
- Talk about the person's abilities, not the test.
- Tie in behaviors with results to help explain performance on tasks.
- Describe patterns of performance across subtests, or across multiple tests.
- Be straightforward in your writing. Assume this is the first time your audience has read an evaluation.

# DON'T FORGET

### Information to Include in Summary and Conclusions Section

- Include summary of referral, key background, and behavioral observation points.
- Summarize the most important interpretations of global scores and highlight strengths and weaknesses.

# CAUTION

## Common Errors to Avoid in Report Writing

- Including inappropriate detail or failing to include pertinent information
- Discussing the test rather than the person's abilities
- Failing to address adequately the reason for referral
- Not supporting hypotheses with adequate data
- Providing information about examinee in the Summary and Conclusion section that has not been presented previously in the other sections of the report
- Failing to synthesize information adequately from all sources (referral source, behavior observations, test results) in summary and conclusions section
- Not providing recommendations that are useful and directly address concerns
- Using poor grammar

## CASE REPORT: JESSICA H., 7-YEAR-OLD FEMALE, REFERRED FOR POSSIBLE ATTENTION-DEFICIT/ HYPERACTIVITY DISORDER

### Kaufman Brief Intelligence Test–Second Edition (KBIT-2) Profile

| Scale | Standard Score | 90% Confidence Interval | Percentile Rank |
|---|---|---|---|
| Verbal | 78 | 71–87 | 7 |
| Nonverbal | 94 | 85–104 | 34 |
| IQ Composite | 84 | 78–91 | 14 |

### Reason for Referral

Jessica was referred by her pediatrician, Dr. Stillwell, due to problems with attention and hyperactivity. According to her mother, Jessica has problems sitting still, concentrating, and following multistep directions. According to her teacher's report, she is often out of her seat and disrupts other children during class. Jessica was evaluated to determine whether she meets criteria for Attention-Deficit/Hyperactivity Disorder and to assist with educational planning at school.

### Background Information

Jessica is a 7-year-old girl who lives with her mother, father, brother (age 4), and sister (age 2). Jessica was the product of a normal pregnancy. She weighed 6 pounds, 8 ounces at birth. There were no perinatal complications. Jessica's mother indicated that she was an alert, cheerful, and affectionate infant. According to the mother's report, Jessica walked at 11 months of age and said her first words at 14 months. She reportedly spoke in sentences at 3 years of age. She has never had a head injury, seizure, lead poisoning, serious illness, or hospitalization. She broke her leg at age 4. She exhibits seasonal allergies and takes Albuteral on an as-needed basis but has no other known physical problems. Family history is positive for speech/language difficulties (maternal side), attention problems (paternal side), and depression (maternal side).

Currently, Jessica is in the first grade at Callwell Elementary School, which is a private independent school in Hillsborough, Illinois. She attended preschool at Causeway School when she was 3 years old and Hillsborough Nursery School at age 4. According to the mother, Jessica seemed immature following kindergarten and, following consultation with the school, the parents agreed for her to repeat kindergarten. According to her mother, Jessica had a difficult time settling down to learn letters and numbers and would often get up and walk away from her schoolwork before it was completed. Her mother reported that Jessica performed better during her second year of kindergarten and gained the academic skills necessary to be promoted to the first grade. According to her mother, Jessica's first-grade teachers report that she exhibits attention problems at school. Due to teacher concerns, Jessica has been moved to the front of the class to help her focus. Her teachers are not reporting academic difficulties at this time; however, she has only been in the first grade for 2 months.

Jessica's mother describes her as a sociable child who has many friendships. She reportedly has one good friend in class as well as friendships with others in the neighborhood. Jessica is reported by her mother to get along well with her siblings. Her mother indicated that Jessica typically is content playing by herself. Jessica enjoys gymnastics, swimming, skiing, and horseback riding as her primary recreational activities. However, the mother reports that Jessica is very careful when participating in physical activities because she is fearful that she might get hurt.

## Behavior Observations

Jessica presented as a casually dressed 7-year-old. She appeared her stated age. She has blue eyes, blonde curly hair, and fair skin. She was a friendly, talkative child and separated from her mother without difficulty. She appeared to put forth her best effort during the evaluation. Problems with attention and impulsivity were noted throughout the evaluation; however, attention difficulties were most apparent on verbal tasks. On verbal tasks, Jessica appeared to be daydreaming and did not answer the examiner's questions. She continued to daydream until her name was called. It was necessary for the examiner to repeat questions frequently, as Jessica often appeared to have forgotten the task at hand. Following some verbal questions, Jessica said, "What?" and asked the examiner to repeat questions. Throughout the evaluation, Jessica was distracted by stimuli in the room. For example, she looked at things under the table. She distracted herself by watching her finger as she ran it up and down the wall by the table. Jessica was out of her seat on several occasions and fidgeted in her chair. Jessica was also impulsive and tried to start tasks before the examiner had finished providing her with directions. Given the consistency of these observations with concerns expressed by her parents and teachers, results of the evaluation are felt to be an accurate reflection of Jessica's typical level of functioning.

## Tests Administered

Kaufman Brief Intelligence Test–Second Edition (KBIT-2)

Conners' Continuous Performance Test–Second Edition (CCPT-II)

Behavior Assessment System for Children–Second Edition (BASC-2): Parent Rating Scale and Teacher Rating Scale, and Structured Developmental History

Behavior Rating Inventory of Executive Function–Parent and Teacher Report (BRIEF)

Parent Interview

## Test Results and Interpretation
### Brief Evaluation of Cognitive Functioning

To obtain an estimate of her global intelligence, Jessica was administered the Kaufman Brief Intelligence Test–Second Edition (KBIT-2). The KBIT-2 is a brief, individually administered measure of verbal and nonverbal intelligence and is comprised of two verbal subtests and one nonverbal subtest. On the KBIT-2, Jessica earned a Verbal Standard Score of 74 (7th percentile), Nonverbal Standard Score of 94 (34th percentile), and IQ Composite of 84 (14th percentile). Because there is a significant difference between Jessica's Verbal and Nonverbal standard scores on the KBIT-2, the IQ Composite should not be interpreted as a meaningful representation of her overall performance. While the 16-point difference between Jessica's below-average verbal and average nonverbal abilities is significant, the difference in abilities is not unusually large for a child her age. Nevertheless, it is better practice to view her verbal and nonverbal abilities separately when reflecting upon her academic aptitude and related skills. The pattern of the observed difference is consistent with behavioral observations of more serious attentional problems on verbal tasks and superior skills in the domain of nonverbal intelligence relative to verbal intelligence. The common occurrence of differences of this magnitude (about 1 in 4 normal children), however, argues that the difference is not of any special diagnostic consequence.

### Behavior Ratings and Executive Functioning

To obtain information regarding Jessica's behavior and emotional functioning in the home and at school, her mother and first-grade teacher, Shana Bellaros, completed the appropriate rating scales from the Behavior Assessment Scale for Children–Second Edition (BASC-2). On the BASC-2, which compares a student's social, emotional, and behavioral functioning in a variety of areas to other children in the same age range, Jessica's mother and her teacher indicated that Jessica exhibits clinically significant and at-risk levels of attention problems, respectively. Both her mother and her teacher indicated that Jessica is almost always easily distracted and has a short attention span. Ms. Bellaros reported problems with hyperactivity falling in the clinically significant range while her mother indicated that she is at-risk for concerns in these areas. Ms. Bellaros indicated that Jessica almost always has trouble staying seated. Both respondents reported problems with poor self-control and impulsivity as occurring on an often basis. In the area of adaptive functioning, Jessica's mother and teacher indicated that she is at-risk for problems with functional communication. Her teacher reported that she is "never" able to describe her feelings accurately, and both respondents indicated that she is sometimes unclear when presenting ideas.

On the Behavior Rating Inventory of Executive Function (BRIEF), a behavior checklist that focuses on executive functions, such as self-regulation, planning, and organization in every day life, Jessica's mother and teacher consistently indicated clinically significant concerns in the area of inhibition (e.g., "often" interrupts others, blurts things out, gets out of the seat at the wrong time) working memory (e.g., "often" has a short attention span, has trouble with tasks that have more than one step), planning and organization (e.g., becomes overwhelmed by large assignments, written work is poorly organized), and self-monitoring of behavior (e.g., becomes too silly, does not realize that certain actions bother others). These problem areas were noted to be consistent with elevations on the BASC-2 Executive Function Scale as well.

Jessica exhibited significant problems on a performance-based test of simple sustained attention (Conners' Continuous Performance Test–Second Edition; CCPT-II) that required her to press the space bar whenever a letter is flashed on a computer screen, *except* for the letter X. Jessica's Clinical Confidence Index (95.6 percent) was consistent with a clinical sample of individuals with identified attention deficits. Consistent with the parent and teacher report as well as behavior observations during the evaluation, there were indicators of significant problems in the areas of inattention, impulsivity, and vigilance. Jessica's responses became slower and more erratic when the interstimulus interval slowed from 1 second to 2 and 4 seconds indicating that Jessica may have problems adjusting to changes in task demands.

## Summary and Conclusions

Jessica is a 7-year-old girl referred for an assessment by her pediatrician. The purpose of the evaluation was to determine whether she meets criteria for a diagnosis of Attention-Deficit/Hyperactivity Disorder and to assist with educational planning at school. Jessica had a normal developmental history. Currently, Jessica is a first-grade student at a private independent school. Because she presented as somewhat immature and had a difficult time settling down to learn, Jessica repeated kindergarten. According to her mother, she made academic progress during her second year of kindergarten.

An estimate of Jessica's overall cognitive abilities was obtained using the KBIT-2. On the KBIT-2, Jessica's average nonverbal abilities were significantly better developed than her below-average verbal abilities. While the difference between her abilities was significant, the difference was not unusually large. That is, Jessica tends to exhibit a relative weakness in her verbal reasoning abilities relative to her nonverbal abilities; however, this cognitive profile is not unusual for a child her age.

Results of behavioral observations, parent and teacher behavior ratings, and a computerized measure of attention indicate that Jessica exhibits significant difficulties with attention and hyperactivity. Problems with attention, hyperactivity, and impulsivity were noted throughout the evaluation. Difficulties with attention were most apparent on verbal tasks. On the BASC-2, Jessica's mother and teacher consistently reported difficulties with attention, hyperactivity, and functional communication. On the BRIEF, her mother and teacher reported that Jessica exhibits difficulties across several areas of executive functioning including inhibition, working memory, planning and organization, and self-monitoring of behavior.

On a computerized measure of attention (CCPT-II), there were indicators of significant problems in the areas of inattention, impulsivity, and vigilance.

In summary, Jessica meets *DSM-IV-TR* criteria for a diagnosis of Attention-Deficit/Hyperactivity Disorder, Combined Type. She exhibits difficulties across two settings in areas of attention, impulsivity, hyperactivity, and executive functioning. Results of a brief measure of intelligence indicated that her cognitive abilities range from the average (nonverbal abilities) to below-average range (verbal abilities). Jessica exhibits a relative weakness in the area of verbal reasoning consistent with reports from her mother and teacher that she is sometimes unclear when presenting ideas and has difficulties describing her feelings accurately.

## Recommendations

1. Given the fact that that her verbal abilities are an area of relative weakness and she exhibits executive functioning deficits, a comprehensive evaluation of Jessica's cognitive and academic abilities is necessary to rule out the possibility of learning difficulties and ensure that she is provided with appropriate services within the educational setting.

2. Based on behavioral observations of difficulty with recall, especially of verbal material (an ability closely aligned with academic success), a comprehensive assessment of memory functions with an instrument such as the Test of Memory and Learning (TOMAL) may be useful in instructional planning.

3. A multimodal approach to treating attention problems is generally recommended, including environmental modifications, counseling, and medication. Jessica's parents should consult with her pediatrician about the potential pros and cons of medical management for her attention disorders.

4. To assist with problems with attention and organization, the following classroom accommodations are recommended:

a. Jessica should continue to be given preferential seating, near the teacher and away from doors and windows to help her attend to lessons. She should be surrounded by peers with good classroom behavior, and placed in a work area with limited distractions.

b. Because sitting in a chair is difficult for her, interactive learning with manipulatives will work well for Jessica. Provide Jessica with both visual aids and verbal instruction to increase the likelihood that she is attending to directions.

c. Given Jessica's attentional issues, it will be important to make sure that her attention is focused before presenting information. She may have trouble sustaining her attention and effort for any extended period and would benefit from occasional breaks. When Jessica's attention has waned, she often becomes unaware of what is going on around her. As a result, when teachers refocus her attention it is important that they also redirect her to task.

d. Avoid multistep directions whenever possible. Provide Jessica with simple, one-step directions, then monitor to make sure that she is completing the task correctly. Provide demonstrations when possible.

e. Due to her problems with attention, Jessica should take tests in a quiet room, free from distractions.

f. Given Jessica's attention deficits, efforts should be made to avoid singling her out or embarrassing her for not paying attention. Rather, she could be "alerted" in advance when she is going to be called on in school, so that she can prepare herself.

g. To assist with organization, it would be helpful to have someone meet with Jessica at the end of the school day to review homework assignments, including making sure she knows the steps involved, where to begin, and what materials are needed.

## CASE REPORT: MARK G., 32-YEAR-OLD MALE, REFERRED FOR ASSESSMENT FOLLOWING RIGHT-HEMISPHERE STROKE

### Wechsler Abbreviated Scale of Intelligence (WASI) Profile

| Scale | IQ | 90% Confidence Interval | Percentile Rank |
|---|---|---|---|
| Verbal Scale | 119 | 113–123 | 90 |
| Performance Scale | 86 | 82–91 | 18 |
| Full Scale-4 | 102 | 99–105 | 55 |

| Subtest | T-Score | Scaled Score | Subtest | T-Score | Scaled Score |
|---|---|---|---|---|---|
| Vocabulary | 69 | 15 | Block Design | 40 | 7 |
| Similarities | 61 | 13 | Matrix Reasoning | 41 | 7 |

### Reason for Referral

Mark G. suffered an ischemic right-hemisphere stroke on March 3, 2006. For the past 5 weeks, he has received speech and language therapy, physical therapy, and cognitive rehabilitation at an inpatient rehabilitation hospital. He was referred for a brief intellectual screening by his neurologist, Dr. Manning, to assess his baseline level of cognitive functioning with special reference to problem-solving skills to assist in discharge planning and outpatient rehabilitation.

### Background Information

Mark appeared oriented and seemed to be a reliable historian. He provided the following history. Mark is a 32-year-old man who lives in St. Joseph, Missouri, with his wife and 3-year-old son. According to Mark, he has never had a head injury, seizure disorder, or serious illness and was generally in good health prior to the stroke. Mark reportedly smokes approximately a half a pack of cigarettes per day. He indicated that he drinks alcoholic beverages in moderation when at social events and will occasionally have a glass of wine with dinner. Mark's father died from a stroke when he was 63. His mother, age 59, reportedly struggles with hypertension. Mark does not have siblings. Family medical and psychiatric history is positive for kidney failure, stroke, hypertension, heart attack, and substance abuse.

For the past 6 years, Mark has worked as a sales representative for a company that sells customized sporting equipment and uniforms. His job requires a great deal of travel and organization, and he is often out of town 3 or 4 days per week. He reportedly relies on his verbal and social skills to promote the company's products and maintain positive business contacts. Mark often gives presentations to large groups of customers. Mark is reportedly well liked and respected by his coworkers. Mark enjoys his job and anticipates returning to work as soon as possible.

Mark graduated high school and attended a 2-year community college. By Mark's report, he earned As and Bs while taking business classes at community college. He worked full-time at an electronics store while taking classes. He considered pursuing a bachelor's degree; however, he decided that he did not want the later burden of additional loans to finance his education.

Following the stroke, Mark exhibits hemiplegia of his left leg and foot. He is currently undergoing physical therapy and has regained partial use of his leg; however, he continues to use a wheelchair at most times. Mark's neuropsychologist indicated that he exhibits mild to moderate problems with attention and fatigues easily. Mark is motivated to return home to be with his family and is encouraged by his progress. He reported that he has felt "down and out" about not being able to walk.

**Behavior Observations**

Mark presented as a friendly 32-year-old male. He appeared his stated age and was of average height and weight. He appeared to put forth his best effort during the evaluation. Mark had difficulties with attention and often asked for items to be repeated. He frequently said, "I'm sorry. Can you ask that again?" Mark had more difficulty on visual-spatial tasks. He became visibly frustrated and sighed loudly on a task that required him to recreate block designs. When the block designs became more difficult, Mark threw the blocks down and said, "I just can't do this." With encouragement from the examiner, he completed all necessary items. Mark was anxious regarding his performance. When the test was over, Mark asked the examiner, "How did I do? Am I going to be okay?" Overall results of this evaluation are felt to be an accurate reflection of Mark's current functioning.

## Tests Administered

Wechsler Abbreviated Scale of Intelligence (WASI)
Beck Depression Inventory–Second Edition (BDI-II)
Clinical Interview

## Test Results and Interpretation
## Brief Evaluation of Cognitive Functioning

Mark was administered the Wechsler Abbreviated Scale of Intelligence (WASI) to obtain an estimate of his global intelligence. The WASI is a brief, individually administered test of a person's intellectual ability that is comprised of 4 subtests and measures both verbal and nonverbal abilities. On the WASI, Mark earned a Full Scale IQ of 102, which classifies his intelligence in the average range and ranks him at the 55th percentile when compared to other adults his age. The chances are 9 out of 10 that his true Full Scale IQ falls within the range of 99–105. However, because there was a significant difference of 33 points between the Verbal and Performance components of his Full Scale IQ, the Full Scale IQ of 102 is rendered essentially meaningless as a summary of such disparate scores makes little psychometric sense. Furthermore, the Verbal versus

Performance discrepancy was found to be abnormally large, and occurring in less than 1 percent of normal individuals. Mark's Verbal IQ of 119 (90th percentile; High Average range) was significantly greater than his Performance IQ of 86 (18th percentile; Low Average). This significant difference indicates that Mark has substantially better verbal intelligence as demonstrated on tasks requiring vocabulary definitions and verbal reasoning than nonverbal intelligence as seen on tasks of visual-spatial problem solving and abstract nonverbal reasoning.

### Brief Assessment of Emotional Functioning

To assess the intensity of his feelings of sadness, Mark was administered the Beck Depression Inventory–Second Edition (BDI-II). The BDI-II is a 21-item inventory that assesses symptoms of depression consistent within the last 2 weeks, with an emphasis on biological markers of depression. Results of the BDI-II indicated that Mark exhibits a mildly elevated level of depression.

### Summary and Conclusions

Mark is a 32-year-old male who suffered an ischemic right-hemisphere stroke on March 3, 2006. As a result of the stroke, Mark suffered hemiplegia of the left leg and foot. During the past 5 weeks, Mark has been at an inpatient rehabilitation hospital receiving speech and language therapy, physical therapy, and cognitive rehabilitation. He has regained partial use of his leg and foot; however, he continues to require the use of a wheelchair. He also exhibits problems with attention and reports feelings of sadness. Mark is married, has a 3-year-old son, and has worked as a sales representative for the last 6 years. He was referred for a brief psychological screening by his neurologist to assess to his cognitive skills and assist with discharge planning. During the evaluation he was friendly and appeared to put forth his best effort. He exhibited difficulties with attention and his frustration tolerance was low on nonverbal tasks.

Mark's intellectual abilities were highly variable ranging from the low-average to high-average range on the WASI. The significant and abnormally large discrepancy between his high-average verbal (SS = 119) and low-average nonverbal abilities (SS = 86) indicates that Mark functions at a substantially higher level in the domain of verbal intelligence than nonverbal intelligence.

Results of a brief screening for depression (BDI-II) indicated that Mark exhibits mildly elevated levels of depression. During the clinical interview he reported that he has felt "down and out" since the stroke. While he has made progress during physical therapy, he continues to need to use a wheelchair. He is reportedly anxious to return to work and his family.

Overall, Mark is an intelligent 32-year-old male who suffered an ischemic right-hemisphere stroke. The brief psychological screening indicated that when compared to his high-average verbal abilities, Mark exhibits a relative weakness in his low-average nonverbal abilities. Given that there is no record of Mark's premorbid level of cognitive functioning, it is not possible to determine whether there has been a decline in his nonverbal abilities as a result of the stroke. Mark exhibits difficulties with attention and fatigue. Finally, Mark exhibits symptoms of depression in the mild range that should be monitored carefully.

## Recommendations

1. Mark will benefit from receiving counseling services to address issues of sadness and frustration and assist with developing effective coping skills. If available, Mark will benefit from participating in a group for individuals within his age range who have suffered a stroke.

2. Because Mark reportedly fatigues easily, he may consider returning to work gradually. For example, he may wish to work

part-time on a trial basis until he gains the required stamina to work for an 8-hour day.

3. Mark should be provided with environmental modifications at work to assist with his attention problems. He will be most productive in an environment that is free from distractions and away from doors and windows. Because he has problems with attention and easily becomes overwhelmed, he will also benefit from occasional, well-placed breaks.

4. If Mark continues to exhibit difficulties with attention once he has returned to work, he may consider rendering the services of a job coach for individuals with attention problems. A mentor may help Mark organize his work space, learn concrete skills and techniques to prioritize tasks, help him map out time blocks needed to finish tasks, and assist with follow through and work completion.

## CASE REPORT: JACK P., 5-YEAR-OLD MALE, REFERRED FOR SCREENING TO RULE OUT SIGNIFICANT DEVELOPMENTAL DELAY

### Reynolds Intellectual Screening Test (RIST) Profile

| Scale | IQ | 90% Confidence Interval | Percentile Rank |
|---|---|---|---|
| RIST Composite Index | 93 | 88–99 | 32 |

| Subtest | T-Score | Percentile Rank |
|---|---|---|
| Guess What (verbal) | 42 | 21 |
| Odd-Item Out (nonverbal) | 48 | 42 |

### Reason for Referral

Jack P. is a 5-year-old male who will be starting kindergarten this fall. Jack was evaluated as part of a routine screening conducted by Sandell's School District to rule out significant developmental delays.

### Background Information

Jack is a 5-year-old boy who lives with his mother and maternal grandparents. His father lives out of state and he has had no contact with him. Jack was the product of a normal pregnancy. He weighed 8 pounds, 4 ounces at birth. He was jaundiced at birth and received phototherapy under bilirubin lights for 2 days. There were no other perinatal complications. Jack's mother reported that Jack was somewhat colicky and difficult to soothe as an infant. Developmental milestones were reportedly achieved within expected time frames. He walked at 13 months and said his first words at 10 months. Jack reportedly spoke in sentences at age 2. He was toilet trained by 4 years of age. Jack fell and hit his head on the fireplace mantel when he was 2 years old and suffered a skull fracture. There is no other history of head injury, seizure, lead poisoning, serious illness, or hospitalization. Jack does not have any allergies and he does not take any medications. Family history is positive for learning problems and anxiety (maternal side).

Jack has never attended preschool or daycare. His grandparents care for him while his mother is at work. Jack's mother reported that his grandparents spend a great deal of time teaching him basic school-readiness skills such as colors, shapes, and the alphabet. He reportedly enjoys learning and responds well to positive reinforcement.

Jack's mother describes him as a shy child who is reluctant to approach other children. Once he makes friendships with children, however, he enjoys playing with others his age. He attends Sunday school classes at church with other children and he occasionally attends play dates with a child of one of his mother's coworkers.

> # CAUTION
>
> As can be seen readily when reviewing the table of test results in the case of Jack (RIST case example), percentile ranks, if presented alone, often exaggerate small score differences near the population mean (see scaled scores and percentile ranks for Guess What and Odd-Item Out). However, they can inappropriately minimize very large score differences at the tails of the distribution. So that your reader is not misled, always include both the standardized or scaled scores along with the percentile ranks and your interpretation of the scores.

## Behavior Observations

Jack presented as a casually dressed 5-year-old. He has brown hair, brown eyes, and a dark complexion. He was extremely timid and did not separate easily from his mother. When she attempted to separate, he grabbed her pant leg and said, "No mama, no." In an attempt to make Jack feel more comfortable, the examiner spent time playing and drawing pictures with Jack while his mother was in the room. When he appeared more at ease, his mother quietly exited the room and the examiner began the assessment. Jack did not initiate conversation throughout the assessment; however, he answered all questions asked of him. He spoke in complete sentences and there was no indication of speech articulation difficulties. Jack initially provided his responses in a whisper. As the evaluation progressed, he used a normal volume. On a couple of occasions, Jack asked, "Where is my mama?" The examiner was able to assure Jack that his mother was just outside the room and he would be reunited with her shortly. There were no indications of problems with attention or hyperactivity. While coloring, it was noted that Jack is right handed and exhibits a mature pencil grip. Overall results are felt to be an accurate reflection of Jack's current level of functioning.

### Tests Administered

> Behavior Assessment System for Children–Second Edition–Parent Rating Scale–Preschool (BASC-2)
> Reynolds Intellectual Screening Test (RIST)
> Bracken Basic Concept Scale–Revised
> Parent Interview

### Test Results and Interpretation
### Brief Screening of Behavioral and Emotional Functioning

Jack's mother completed the Behavior Assessment Scale for Children–Second Edition (BASC-2) Parent Rating Scale to obtain information regarding Jack's behavioral and emotional functioning in the home. The BASC-2 compares a student's social, emotional, and behavioral functioning in a variety of areas to other students in the same age range. On the BASC-2, Jack's mother indicated that he is at-risk for problems with withdrawal, adaptability, and social skills. More specifically, she endorsed items indicating that he sometimes avoids other children and clings to his parent in strange surroundings. He does not adjust well to new surroundings or changes in routine. In the area of social skills, he never offers to help other children and he does not compliment others.

## Brief Evaluation of Cognitive Functioning

To obtain an estimate of his general intellectual development, Jack was administered the Reynolds Intellectual Screening Test (RIST). The RIST is a brief, individually administered measure of intelligence that is comprised of one verbal and one nonverbal subtest, each heavily focused on the development of reasoning skills in the domains of crystallized (verbal) and fluid (nonverbal) intelligence. On the RIST, Jack earned a RIST Composite Index of 93 (32nd percentile), indicating that his overall cognitive abilities are in the average range compared to same-age peers. The chances are 9 out of 10 that his true RIST Composite Index falls in the range of scores from 88 to 99. There was no suggestion of uneven development in the verbal and nonverbal domains in his subtest scores.

## Brief Evaluation of Academic Skills

To assess his school-readiness skills, Jack was administered the first six subtests of the Bracken Basic Concept Scale–Revised. These subtests assess a child's knowledge of colors, letters, numbers/counting, sizes, comparisons, and shapes. Jack's knowledge of basic school-readiness skills was average (Bracken School Readiness Composite SS = 91, 27th percentile) compared to same-age peers.

## Summary and Conclusions

Jack is a 5-year-old male who was referred for testing as part of a routine screening conducted by Sandell's School District to rule out significant developmental delays before starting kindergarten this fall. Jack's birth and developmental history were unremarkable. Jack suffered a skull fracture at age 2 years. There was no other report of head injury, seizure, lead poisoning, serious illness, or hospitalization. He has never attended day care or preschool. His maternal grandparents care for him while his mother is at work. According to his mother, Jack is shy around other children but enjoys playing and interacting with children once he feels comfortable. Jack was initially resistant to separate from his mother during the evaluation; however, once he felt more comfortable with the examiner, he separated without difficulty and results of the evaluation were considered valid.

To obtain information regarding his social, emotional, and behavioral functioning, Jack's mother completed the BASC-2 parent rating scale. Consistent with information obtained during the parent interview and behavior observations, Jack's mother endorsed items indicating that he is at-risk for problems with withdrawal, adaptability, and social skills. Jack tends to be a shy child who prefers to spend time with familiar people and surroundings. Results of brief intelligence testing using the RIST indicate that Jack's cognitive abilities are within the average range for a child his age. In addition, Jack's knowledge of basic school-readiness skills was average compared to his same-age peers.

In summary, Jack's cognitive and academic abilities are within the average range and there is no indication of significant developmental delay at this time. As is necessary with all school-age children, his progress should be closely monitored to ensure his academic success. Jack tends to be a shy child and extra care should be taken to ensure a successful transition to kindergarten.

### Recommendations

1. Jack will benefit from visiting his new school a few times before the academic year begins. It also will be helpful for him to become acquainted with students from his class before school begins. To facilitate this, his mother may arrange play dates with students this summer.
2. Jack will benefit from being paired with a buddy during the new school year that may show him around the school and help him feel comfortable.

## CASE REPORT: ASHLEY B., 9-YEAR-OLD FEMALE, REFERRED FOR ASSESSMENT FOR GIFTED AND TALENTED PROGRAM

### Wide Range Intelligence Test (WRIT) Profile

| Scale | IQ | 90% Confidence Interval | Percentile Rank |
|-------|-----|-------------------------|-----------------|
| Verbal | 131 | 123–135 | 98 |
| Visual | 125 | 117–130 | 95 |
| General | 133 | 126–137 | 99 |

| Subtest | Standard Score | Subtest | Standard Score |
|---------|----------------|---------|----------------|
| Verbal Analogies | 126 | Matrices | 119 |
| Vocabulary | 131 | Diamonds | 123 |

### Reason for Referral

Ashley B. is a 9-year-old female who is in the 3rd grade at Pershing Elementary School. She was referred for an evaluation by her classroom teacher, Janet Altieri, to determine whether she is an appropriate candidate for the school's gifted and talented program.

### Background Information

Ashley is a 9-year-old girl who lives with her mother, father, and twin sisters (age 12). She was the product of a normal pregnancy. Ashley weighed 7 pounds, 3 ounces at birth. There were no perinatal complications. Ashley was reportedly affectionate, cheerful, and social as an infant. Developmental milestones were achieved within expected time frames. There was no history of head injury, seizure, lead poisoning, serious illness, or hospitalization. Ashley is allergic to chocolate and beef. Family history is positive for autism (paternal side) and attention problems (maternal side).

Ashley attended preschool when she was 3 and 4 years old. She has attended Pershing Elementary from kindergarten through third grade. According to Ms. Altieri, Ashley is considered to be one of the brightest students in the third grade. She is eager to learn and enjoys challenges. She enjoys reading and is currently reading material at the fifth-grade level. When not at school, Ashley enjoys taking tap dance lessons, working in the rose garden with her mother, and drawing. In social areas, Ashley has two close friends in her class and gets along well with others. She is often chosen as a leader and encourages others to try their best.

## Behavior Observations

Ashley presented as a well-dressed 9-year-old. She has brown hair, green eyes, and is somewhat small in stature for her given age. Eye contact was appropriate. She was friendly and confident during the evaluation and eagerly initiated conversation with the examiner. She talked about an upcoming tap dance recital and showed the examiner a demonstration of her routine. She appeared to put forth her best during the evaluation. There were no indications of problems with attention or hyperactivity. Overall, results of the evaluation are felt to be an accurate reflection of Ashley's current level of functioning.

## Tests Administered

Wide Range Intelligence Test (WRIT)
Parent Interview

## Test Results and Interpretation
## Brief Screening of Cognitive Functioning

To obtain an estimate of her global intelligence, Ashley was administered the Wide Range Intelligence Test (WRIT). The WRIT is a brief, individually administered measure of intelligence that is comprised of two subtests that measure verbal abilities and two subtests that assess visual skills. On the WRIT, Ashley earned a General IQ of 133, which classifies her overall intelligence in the very superior range and ranks her at the 99th percentile when compared to other children her age. The chances are 9 out of 10 that her true General Scale IQ falls within the range of 126–137. She earned a Verbal IQ of 131 (98th percentile; very superior) and a Visual IQ of 125 (95th percentile; superior). The six-point difference between her verbal and visual abilities was not statistically significant, indicating that her abilities are essentially equally well developed. Furthermore, there were no significant subtest score differences, indicating that her abilities were evenly demonstrated across verbal and visual subtests.

## Summary and Conclusions

Ashley is a 9-year-old student at Pershing Elementary School who was referred by her third-grade teacher, Janet Altieri, to determine whether she meets entrance criteria for a Gifted and Talented program available at her school. Ashley has attended Pershing Elementary from kindergarten through third grade. She is considered among the brightest children in the third grade and excels in her studies. She is reportedly well liked and is often chosen as a leader. When not at school, she enjoys tap dancing, gardening, and drawing.

Results of brief intelligence testing using the WRIT indicate that Ashley's overall cognitive abilities were in the very superior range compared to other children her age. Her verbal and visual abilities were in the very superior and superior range, respectively, and are somewhat evenly developed.

In summary, Ashley's overall cognitive abilities were in the very superior range. As eligibility for the district's program for the intellectually gifted is set at a general IQ of 125 or higher, Ashley's cognitive abilities as assessed on the WRIT indicate a very high probability of qualifying. In addition to superior cognitive abilities, Ashley reportedly exhibits good leadership skills and is active in extracurricular activities. As such, Ashley is likely to make a good candidate for the Gifted and Talented program.

## 🦫 TEST YOURSELF 🦫

1. **List 5 pieces of information that should be included in the Identifying Information section of the report.**

2. **In the Referral section of the report, you should include all of the following except**

   (a) the referral question.

   (b) the name and position of the person who referred the examinee for testing.

   (c) a statement about the validity of test results.

   (d) possible concerns of parent, caregiver, teacher, or examinee.

3. **In the Referral section of the report, it is not necessary to document previous diagnoses because this information may bias the audience's interpretation of test results.** True or False?

4. **Which of the following should be included in the Background section of a case report?**

   (a) examinee's level of cooperativeness during testing

   (b) developmental history

   (c) summary of previous evaluation(s)

   (d) both b and c

5. **When providing information in the Behavior Observations section of the report, it is important to note unusual behaviors that were noticed during the assessment?** True or False?

6. **In addition to describing samples of the examinee's appearance and behavior, the Behavior Observation section of the report should include:**

   (a) medical and psychiatric history

   (b) the referral question

   (c) a statement about the validity of test results

   (d) summary of test results

7. **Which of the following types of scores should not be included in case reports?**

   (a) percentile rank

   (b) raw score

   (c) standard score

   (d) scaled score

**8. Which information should be included in the Test Results and Interpretation section?**

  (a) full name of tests administered and what they measure

  (b) IQs, Index scores, percentile ranks, and descriptive ranges

  (c) discussion of the examinee's pattern of performance across subtests or measures

  (d) all of the above

**9. It is appropriate to mention information in the Summary and Conclusions section of the report that has not previously been discussed.** True or False?

**10. List 3 common errors that examiners often make when writing case reports.**

  (a) _____

  (b) _____

  (c) _____

*Answers:* 1. See Don't Forget 6.1; 2. c; 3. False; 4. d; 5. True; 6. c; 7. b; 8. d; 9. False; 10. See Caution

# References

Axelrod, B. N. (2002). Validity of the Wechsler Abbreviated Scale of Intelligence and other very short forms of estimating intellectual functioning. *Assessment, 9*(1), 17–23.

Cohen, J., Cohen, P., West, S. G., & Aiken, L. S. (2003). *Applied multiple regression correlation analysis for the behavioral sciences.* Mahwah, NJ: Erlbaum.

Doppelt, J. E. (1956). Estimating the full scale score on the Wechsler Adult Intelligence Scale from scores on four subtests. *Journal of Consulting Psychology, 20*(1), 63–66.

Fish, J. (1990). IQ terminology: Modifications of current schemes. *Journal of Psychoeducational Assessment, 8*(4), 527–530.

Fletcher-Janzen, E., & Reynolds, C. R. (Eds.). (2003). *Childhood disorders diagnostic desk reference.* New York: Wiley.

Goldstein, S., & Reynolds, C. R. (Eds.). (1999). *Handbook of neurodevelopmental and genetic disorders in children.* New York: Guilford.

Glutting, J., Adams, W., & Sheslow, D. (2000). *Wide range intelligence test.* Odessa, FL: Psychological Assessment Resources.

Gorsuch, R. L. (1983, August). *The theory of continuous norming.* Paper presented at the meeting of the American Psychological Association, Anaheim, CA.

Guilford, J. P., & Fruchter, B. (1978). *Fundamental statistics in psychology and education* (6th ed.). New York: McGraw-Hill.

Hays, J. R., Reas, D. L., & Shaw, J. B. (2002). Concurrent validity of the Wechsler Abbreviated Scale of Intelligence and the Kaufman Brief Intelligence Test among psychiatric inpatients. *Psychological Reports, 90*(2), 355–359.

Kamphaus, R. W. (2001). *Clinical assessment of children's intelligence, second edition.* Boston: Allyn & Bacon.

Kamphaus, R. W., & Frick, P. J. (2002). *Clinical assessment of child and adolescent personality.* Boston: Allyn & Bacon.

Kaufman, A. S. (1990). *Assessing adolescent and adult intelligence.* Boston: Allyn & Bacon.

Kaufman, A. S., Ishikuma, T., & Kaufman-Packer, J. L. (1991). Amazingly short forms of the WAIS-R. *Journal of Psychoeducational Assessment, 9,* 4–15.

Kaufman, A. S., & Kaufman, N. L. (1990). *Kaufman Brief Intelligence Test.* Circle Pines, MN: AGS Publishing.

Kaufman, A. S., & Kaufman, N. L. (2004a). *Kaufman Assessment Battery for Children, second edition.* Circle Pines, MN: AGS Publishing.

Kaufman, A. S., & Kaufman, N. L. (2004b). *Kaufman Brief Intelligence Test–Second edition.* Circle Pines, MN: AGS Publishing.

Kaufman, A. S., & Kaufman, N. L. (2004c). *Kaufman Test of Educational Achievement–Second edition, comprehensive form.* Circle Pines, MN: AGS Publishing.

Kaufman, A. S., & Lichtenberger, E. O. (2002). *Assessing adolescent and adult Intelligence* (2nd ed.). Boston: Allyn & Bacon.

Kaufman, A. S., & Lichtenberger, E. O. (2006*). Assessing adolescent and adult intelligence, third edition.* New York: Wiley.

Kellogg, C. E., & Morton, N. W. (1999). *Beta III.* San Antonio, TX: The Psychological Corporation.

King, L. A., & King, D. W. (1982). Wechsler short forms: A brief status report. *Psychology in the Schools, 19,* 433–438.

McNemar, Q. (1950). On abbreviated Wechsler-Bellevue scales. *Journal of Consulting Psychology, 14,* 79–81.

Meyer, M. P. (2001). Use of the Wechsler Abbreviated Scale of Intelligence in a vocational rehabilitation sample. *Dissertation Abstracts International: Section B: The Sciences and Engineering, 61*(12-B), 6713.

Nunnally, J. C. (1978). *Psychometric theory* (2nd ed.). New York: McGraw-Hill.

Prifitera, A., Weiss, L. G., & Saklofske, D. H. (1998). The WISC-III in context. In A. Prifitera & D. H. Saklofske (Eds.), *WISC-III clinical use and interpretation: Scientist-practitioner perspectives* (pp. 1–39). San Diego, CA: Academic Press.

The Psychological Corporation (1992). *Wechsler Individual Achievement Test.* San Antonio, TX: Author.

The Psychological Corporation (1999). *Wechsler Abbreviated Scale of Intelligence.* San Antonio, TX: Author.

Raiford, S. E., Rolfhus, E., Weiss, L. G., & Coalson, D. (2005). *General Ability Index* (WISC-IV Technical Report No. 4). Retrieved March 15, 2005 from http://harcourtassessment.com/haiweb/Cultures/enUS/dotCom/WISC-IV.com/Product+Information/WISC-IV+Technical+Reports.htm

Reynolds, C. R. (1979). Should we screen preschoolers? *Contemporary Educational Psychology, 4,* 175–181.

Reynolds, C. R. (1985). Critical measurement issues in learning disabilities. *Journal of Special Education, 18,* 451–476.

Reynolds, C. R., & Kamphaus, R. W. (2003a). *Reynolds intellectual screening test.* Odessa, FL: Psychological Assessment Resources.

Reynolds, C. R., & Kamphaus, R. W. (2003b). *Reynolds intellectual assessment scales.* Odessa, FL: Psychological Assessment Resources.

Reynolds, C. R., & Kamphaus, R. W. (2004). *Behavior assessment system for children, second edition.* Circle Pines, MN: American Guidance Service.

Reynolds, C. R., Willson, V. L., & Clark, P. L. (1983). A four-test short form of the WAIS-R for clinical screening. *Clinical Neuropsychology, 5*(3), 111–116.

Rourke, B. P. (1998). Significance of verbal-performance discrepancies for subtypes of children with learning disabilities: Opportunities for the WISC-III. In A. Prifitera & D. H. Saklofske (Eds.), *WISC-III clinical use and interpretation: Scientist-practitioner perspectives* (pp. 139–156). San Diego, CA: Academic Press.

Ryan, J. J., & Brown, K. I. (2005). Enhancing the clinical utility of the WASI: Reliabilities of discrepancy scores and supplemental tables for profile analysis. *Journal of Psychoeducational Assessment, 23*(2), 140–145.

Ryan, J. J., Carruthers, C. A., Miller, L. J., Souheaver, G. T., Gontkovsky, S. T., & Zehr, M. D. (2003). Exploratory factor analysis of the Wechsler Abbreviated Scale of Intelligence (WASI) in adult standardization and clinical samples. *Applied Neuropsychology, 10*(4), 252–256.

Sadock, B., & Sadock, S. (Eds.). (2000). *Kalpan and Sadock's comprehensive textbook of psychiatry, seventh edition.* Philadelphia: Lippincott Williams and Wilkins.

Saklofske, D. H., & Schwean-Kowalchuk, V. L. (1992). Influences on testing and test results. In M. Zeidner & R. Most (Eds.), *Psychological testing: An inside view* (pp. 89–118). Palo Alto, CA: Consulting Psychologists Press.

Sattler, J. M. (1988). *Assessment of children* (3rd ed.). San Diego, CA: Author.

Sattler, J. M. (2001). *Assessment of children: Cognitive applications.* San Diego, CA: Author.

Satz, P., & Mogel, S. (1962). An abbreviation of the WAIS for clinical use. *Journal of Clinical Psychology, 18,* 77–79.

Silverstein, A. B. (1982). Two- and four-subtest short forms of the Wechsler Adult Intelligence Scale–Revised. *Journal of Consulting and Clinical Psychology, 50*(3), 415–418.

Smith, G. T., McCarthy, D. M., & Anderson, K. G. (2000). On the sins of short form development. *Psychological Assessment, 12*(1), 102–111.

Stano, J. F. (2004). Test review. *Rehabilitation Counseling Bulletin, 48*(1), 56–57.

Thompson, A. P. (1987). Methodological issues in the clinical evaluation of two- and four-subtest short forms of the WAIS-R. *Journal of Clinical Psychology, 43*(1), 142–144.

Wechsler, D. (1991). *Wechsler Intelligence Scale for Children–Third edition.* San Antonio, TX: The Psychological Corporation.

Wechsler, D. (1997). *Wechsler Adult Intelligence Scale–Third edition.* San Antonio, TX: The Psychological Corporation.

Wechsler, D. (2003). *Wechsler Intelligence Scale for Children–Fourth edition.* San Antonio, TX: The Psychological Corporation.

Wilkinson, G. S. (1993). *Wide Range Achievement Test–3rd edition.* Wilmington, DE: Wide Range.

Wonderlic, Inc. (1999). *Wonderlic personnel test.* Libertyville, IL: Author.

Zachary, R. (1986). *Shipley Institute of Living Scale: Revised manual.* Los Angeles: Western Psychological Services.

Zachary, R., & Gorsuch, R. L. (1985). Continuous norming: Implications for the WAIS-R. *Journal of Clinical Psychology, 41,* 86–94.

# Annotated Bibliography

American Educational Research Association, American Psychological Association, & the National Council on Measurement in Education (1999). *Standards for educational and psychological testing.* Washington, DC: Author.

*This sixth version of the* Standards *represents by far the most massive and thorough revision of the* Standards *ever prepared. It is featured here for two reasons: (1) these* Standards *apply to brief intelligence tests, and, (2) they contain a comprehensive reconceptualization of the concept of validity that is not widely understood even this many years post-publication. Additionally, the* Standards *have been reviewed and adopted by most major membership organizations in the field of psychology and also have been adopted by a number of state licensing boards as part of their rules of practice. The* Standards *also serve as a useful text to understanding how tests should be developed, the documentation that should be provided by test developers and publishers, and discussions of the rights and responsibilities of test users. In addition to excellent chapters on psychometrics (e.g., reliability, validity, scaling), the* Standards *also address the difficult issues of fairness in testing, testing of the linguistically and culturally diverse examinee, and testing individuals with disabilities. In addition to presenting standards of practice in each of these areas, the* Standards *provides an excellent discussion of the concepts underlying each of these principles and standards. These discussions are uniformly valuable in understanding sound practices in all forms of educational and psychological testing. The* Standards *should be read, understood, and periodically reviewed by all individuals involved in testing.*

Fletcher-Janzen, E., & Reynolds, C. R. (Eds.). (2002). *Diagnostic reference manual of childhood disorders.* New York: Wiley.

*This edited work is a compilation of information that is disorder-specific and formatted consistently across all disorders represented. For approximately 800 disorders, ranging from obscure problems such as Soto's syndrome to more common disorders like Tourette's syndrome, phenylketonuria, and galactosemia, various experts present the natural history and etiology of each disorder, diagnostic keys, basic treatment approaches, expected outcomes, and implications for special education intervention. Physical, cognitive (including intellectual), emotional, and behavioral aspects of each disorder are noted and special attention is given to improving diagnostic accuracy.*

Hambleton, R., & Li, S. (2006). Translation and adaptation issues and methods for educational and psychological tests. In C. Frisby & C. R. Reynolds (Eds.), *Comprehensive handbook of multicultural school psychology* (pp. 881–903). New York: Wiley.

*Often it seems necessary to translate, adapt, or in some way modify an existing test for application to culturally diverse populations. Brief intelligence tests are no exception, especially when used in large-scale screening processes. However, making changes in a way that maximizes or preserves (to the extent possible) the psychometric characteristics of the original test is not simple. Hambleton and Li provide in this chapter a review of many of the potential pitfalls in making such adaptations as well as providing clear guidelines for day-to-day practice. After a review of the common myths associated with translations and adaptations, Hambleton and Li give a step-by-step guide to best practice in making these changes. This is followed by a presentation and discussion of the Guidelines for Test Adaptation of the International Test Commission. Overall, Hambleton and Li have provided an excellent discussion of problems and issues, and then given the current state-of-the-art solution to test adaptation.*

Kamphaus, R. W. (2001). *Clinical assessment of children's intelligence* (2nd ed.). New York: Springer.

*This book is a comprehensive treatise on the theoretical and practical aspects of intelligence testing that provides a deep conceptual understanding of issues related to test selection and use. Topics such as test use; theories of intelligence; ethnic, gender, and cultural bias; screeners; report writing; test interpretation; and diagnostic issues are covered in great detail. Kamphaus brings a wealth of both academic and personal clinical expertise to bear on these topics in what is an excellent textbook as well as an ongoing reference work for anyone engaged in intelligence.*

Kamphaus, R. W., & Campbell, J. C. (2006). *Psychodiagnostic assessment of children: Dimensional and categorical methods.* New York: Wiley.

*This new book provides a comprehensive view of the diagnostic process including the use of intelligence test data for the diagnosis of Autism Spectrum Disorders, Reading Disabilities, Mental Retardation, Traumatic Brain Injury, and numerous other syndromes of childhood. Kamphaus and Campbell also review the role of testing in the use of DSM-IV, IDEIA, and related categorical systems and contrast these approaches to emerging methods of dimensional diagnosis. Clearly, dimensional models of diagnosis of emotional and behavioral disorders seems to make a great deal more sense than categorical models derived principally from medical views of the presence of pathogens or injuries or dysfunctional organs or organ systems. This book is a must read for those engaged in clinical diagnosis in any area of psychology.*

Kamphaus, R. W., Reynolds, C. R., & Imperato-McCammon, C. (1999). Roles of diagnosis and classification in school psychology. In C. R. Reynolds & T. B. Gutkin (Eds.), *The handbook of school psychology* (3rd ed., pp. 292–306). New York: Wiley.

*Diagnosis and classification of children into diagnostic groups to receive services is a perpetual controversy in school psychology and related disciplines. This chapter reviews selected issues of diagnosis, including the uses of diagnostic systems, current dominant systems of classification in childhood psychopathology, the classification system of the IDEA, and dimensional systems typically of empirical derivation. The effects commonly attributed to diagnosis are reviewed, as well as some potential problems of the failure to diagnose. The concept of assessment as the ongoing development of an understanding of the individual is contrasted with the simple eligibility decisions prevalent in schools. The link between diagnosis and treatment is emphasized.*

Kaufman, A. S., & Lichtenberger, E. O. (2006). *Assessing adolescent and adult intelligence, 3rd ed.* New York: Wiley.

*The third edition of this outstanding text is virtually identical to the second edition published in 2002, the major change being the addition of 4 appendixes related to recent information concerning the interpretation of the Wechsler Adult Intelligence Scale–Third Edition (WAIS-III). Unfortunately it contains no information on intelligence tests published for adolescents and adults since 2002 (e.g., the RIAS published in 2003). However, for individuals who use the WAIS-III, this classic text remains indispensable. It is simply the most thorough and useful treatise on the WAIS-III that has ever been produced. It also has informative discussions of the differential effects of aging on various aspects of intelligence. The volume also includes a description and interpretive strategies for application of the Kaufman Adolescent and Adult Intelligence Test. A final chapter provides coverage of several brief intelligence tests published prior to 2002. With the exception of lacking coverage of measures published since 2002, Kaufman and Lichtenberger's text is superb and should be read by anyone who conducts comprehensive intellectual assessments of adults.*

Keith, T. Z., & Reynolds, C. R. (2003). Measurement and design issues in child assessment research. In C. R. Reynolds & R. W. Kamphaus (Eds.), *Handbook of psychological and educational assessment of children, Vol. 1: Intelligence, aptitude and achievement* (pp. 79–111). New York: Guilford.

*In this chapter the authors denote problems and solutions to many of the difficult issues encountered in child assessment research. The focus of the work being on measurement, statistical, and research design issues, fully 80 percent or more of the chapter applies to assessment research with any age group. The authors provide guidance in how to design assessment research that is consistent with both theory and practice issues. Research methodologies are presented for common studies of the reliability and validity of test scores using traditional variance definitions, varying methods of factor analysis, and multiple regression, path analysis, and structural equation modeling. The application of the latter three methods to questions of clinical diagnosis and classification is emphasized. The oft-underestimated effects of shrinkage (and their estimation from various research designs) in diagnostic research that culminates in, at times, gross overestimates of classification or hit rates is reviewed along with the need for crossvalidation. Traditional as well as innovative approaches for detecting nominal sources of bias in testing is treated in reasonable detail. Examples of applications of most of the methods discussed are provided, improving the readability of what at times is dense material. This chapter is recommended not just for those who do, or wish to do, high quality, relevant research in child assessment, but also for consumers of research so they can read critically and comprehend work presented in test manuals and journal articles more thoroughly.*

Ochoa, H. S. (2003). Assessment of culturally and linguistically diverse children. In C. R. Reynolds & R. W. Kamphaus (Eds.), *Handbook of psychological and educational assessment of children, Vol. 1: Intelligence, aptitude and achievement* (pp. 563–583). New York: Guilford.

*The number of individuals living and working in the United States who are from outside the mainstream, traditional cultures of the United States continues to grow rapidly. The assessment of all persons who are culturally or linguistically divergent from the standardization samples of tests or the background of the examiner present us with special challenges. The use of brief intelligence tests with these individuals is no exception and indeed may require even greater care and expertise. In this chapter, Ochoa provides a comprehensive review of the issues and stumbling blocks that surround the proper assessment of culturally and linguistically diverse students. His focus is on critical issues that affect day-to-day practice in conducting such assessments with an emphasis on assessment of intelligence and academic achievement. Solutions are suggested as well as areas for future research where our current level of knowledge is meager.*

Reynolds, C. R. (1979). Should we screen preschoolers? *Contemporary Educational Psychology, 4,* 175–181.

*Despite the age of this paper, reading it now reveals its remarkable currency. The issues and controversies related to early screening for cognitive disorders, special education services, and potential effects of formal versus informal labels applied to children at these young ages are little changed in the past 3 decades. Herein, Reynolds reviews the controversies as well as the arguments for and against early screening and classification. The issue of labeling effects from both formal diagnostic processes and the informal, often pejorative, labeling occurring as a result of the natural course of human interaction are reviewed. Ultimately, Reynolds concluded that the accurate application of formal diagnostic classification and the benefits of early intervention outweigh the potential negative effects of early classification.*

Reynolds, C. R., Livingston, R. B., & Willson, V. L. (2006). *Measurement and assessment in education.* Boston: Allyn & Bacon.

*In this textbook, Reynolds et al. review current psychometrics from an applied perspective with an emphasis on using tests in schools. Chapter 13, "the use of aptitude tests in schools," will be of special interest to readers of the current Essentials book. In this chapter, Reynolds et al. provide a brief history of intelligence testing and then focus on the major tests of aptitude and intelligence currently in use in the schools. Group tests are reviewed in detail here and sample printouts of the computer-scoring typically received by schools for these tests are provided with an explanation of how to read and interpret these printouts. In other chapters, Reynolds et al. provide an explanation of the 1999 Standards reconceptualization of validity and related discussions of reliability, linking these issues to past conceptualizations. The authors also present a discussion of the major controversies surrounding the use of aptitude measures in the schools, including IQ tests, and an explanation of the so-called Flynn Effect (i.e., the systematic worldwide increase in IQ over the last near-century).*

Riccio, C. A., Reynolds, C. R., & Lowe, P. A. (2001). *Clinical applications of continuous performance tests: Measuring attention and impulsive responding in children and adults.* New York: Wiley.

*Continuous performance tests (CPTs) have been proffered as a panacea for diagnosis of ADHD. This book-length treatment of the now-enormous 40-year history of CPT presents a different perspective on how the tests should be used. Riccio, Reynolds, and Lowe review information from over 400 studies involving CPTs and various diagnostic groups, reporting that CPTs are highly sensitive performance-based measures of attention problems and impulsive responding. This makes the CPT a useful adjunct to impressionistic behavior-rating scales. The authors begin with a tutorial on the neurobiology of attention, discussing both neurochemistry and neuropsychological models of executive control. Next, they describe the major paradigms surrounding CPTs suggested for clinical use and the differences between them. The volume presents a review of technical adequacy and standardization of each major paradigm, followed by chapters on the sensitivity and specificity of CPTs in the diagnosis of disorders of children and adults. The relationship of CPTs to other tests is also reviewed and the uses of CPTs in diagnosis and in monitoring treatment effects, especially psychopharmacological effects, are noted. This work provides a reference source for everyone who evaluates children with behavioral problems associated with disorders of attention, executive control, or both, in either using CPTs as a component of the diagnostic process or interpreting reports from those who do. As Hynd notes in the foreword, CPTs can vary considerably, and performance can be impaired by a host of disorders, making a comprehensive reference such as this text not simply useful, but necessary.*

Sandoval, J., & Irvin, M. (2003). Legal and ethical issues in the assessment of children. In C. R. Reynolds & R. W. Kamphaus (Eds.), *Handbook of psychological and educational assessment of children, Vol. 1: Intelligence, aptitude and achievement* (pp. 58–78). New York: Guilford.

*There are numerous pitfalls lurking for those who use tests with examinees of all ages and many are legal and/or ethical in nature. In this book chapter, Sandoval and Irvin review the majority of such issues related to children. They address such topics as due process, equal protection, ethnic bias, educational tracking via test scores, testing accommodations for individuals with disabilities, privacy concerns, informed consent, and the reporting of test results in addition to numerous other topics. Of particular interest, they address the issue of conflicts one may encounter between laws and ethics as well as how to consider and interpret ethics guidelines when encountering problems that may be new or addressed only tangentially. All such problems and issues seem perennial in nature and while some have clear, resolute answers, some do not. Sandoval and Irvin do a nice job of distinguishing the two and in discussing the many issues that can arise, providing practical, insightful guidance to even the journeyman practitioner in most instances.*

Smith, G. T., McCarthy, D. M., & Anderson, K. G. (2000). On the sins of short-form development. *Psychological Assessment, 12*(1), 102–111.

*Here Smith and colleagues review briefly what they consider to be the "overly optimistic views" of the transfer of validity evidence from a parent form of a test to a short form of the same instrument. They argue that, among other things, validity research on a short-form needs to be calculated independently of reliance on the validity of the parent form from which the short-form was derived. Subsequent to this review, they detail some 11 sins (methodological errors or at least serious shortcomings) characterizing most efforts of researchers who develop short forms of intelligence and other psychological tests. Their critique is reasonably thorough and quite useful. The paper closes on a more positive note as the authors present a series of nine sequential steps for those who develop short forms of tests. Smith et al. argue that if these steps are followed, ". . . then researchers will be in a strong position to argue that their short-form is a reliable, valid alternative to a fuller more comprehensive assessment" (p. 110).*

# Index

# About the Authors

**Susan Homack, PhD,** earned her Doctoral Degree from Texas A&M University in 2005 with a major in School Psychology and minor in Pediatric Neuropsychology. She served an internship with an emphasis in pediatric neuropsychology within the Department of Behavioral Medicine at Miami Children's Hospital working primarily with children with intractable epilepsy and brain cancer. She completed a postdoctoral fellowship in pediatric neuropsychology at North Shore Children's Hospital in Salem, Massachusetts. Dr. Homack currently holds a position in neuropsychology services at Our Children's House at Baylor in Dallas, Texas, where she conducts evaluations on children and adolescents with developmental disabilities and provides cognitive rehabilitation services to children with Traumatic Brain Injury. Dr. Homack's primary research interests include psychological assessment, Attention-Deficit/Hyperactivity Disorder, and Traumatic Brain Injury. She has published manuscripts in a variety of journals in the field including *Archives of Clinical Neuropsychology, Journal of Attention Disorders,* and *Journal of Clinical and Experimental Neuropsychology,* in addition to making frequent presentations at various state and national conferences.

**Cecil R. Reynolds, PhD,** earned his Doctoral Degree from the University of Georgia in 1978 under the tutelage of Alan Kaufman, with a major in School Psychology and minors in Statistics and in Clinical Neuropsychology. Prior to joining the Texas A&M University faculty in 1981, Dr. Reynolds was a faculty member at the University of Nebraska–Lincoln, where he served as Associate Director and Acting Director of the Buros Institute of Mental Measurement, after writing the grants and proposals to move the Institute to Nebraska following the death of its founder, Oscar Buros. He is the author of more than 300 scholarly publications and author or editor of more than 40 books including *The Clinician's Guide to the BASC, Clinical Applications of Continuous Performance Tests, The Handbook of School Psychology,* and the *Handbook of Clinical Child Neuropsychology.* He is the author of several widely used tests of personality and behavior including the *Behavior Assessment System for Children* and the *Revised Children's Manifest Anxiety Scale.* He is also senior author of the *Test of Memory and Learning,* the *Clinical Assessment Scales for the Elderly,* and coauthor of several computerized test interpretation systems. He is senior author of the *Reynolds Intellectual Assessment Scales* (RIAS). He maintained a clinical practice treating trauma victims and individuals with Traumatic Brain Injury for 25 years before retiring from clinical work at the end of 2003.

Dr. Reynolds holds a diplomate in Clinical Neuropsychology from the American Board of Professional Neuropsychology, of which he is also a past president, and was a diplomate in School Psychology of the American Board of Professional Psychology, prior to retiring his diplomate in 2004. He is a past president of the National Academy of Neuropsychology and APA Divisions 5 (Evaluation, Measurement, and Statistics), 40 (Clinical Neuropsychology), and 16 (School Psychology). He served as Editor of *Archives of Clinical Neuropsychology* (1990–2002), the official journal of the National Academy of Neuropsychology, and serves on the editorial boards of 11 other journals. He is the current Editor of *Applied Neuropsychology* and Associate Editor of *School Psychology Quarterly.* Dr. Reynolds has received multiple national awards recognizing him for excellence in research including the Lightner Witmer Award and early career awards from APA Divisions 5 and 15. He is a corecipient of the Society for the Psychological Study of Social Issues Robert Chin Award. In 1999, Dr. Reynolds received the Senior Scientist Award from APA Division 16 (School Psychology). In 2000, he received the National Academy of Neuropsychology's Distinguished Neuropsychologist Award, the Academy's highest award for research accomplishments. He received the NASP 2003 Lifetime Achievement Award in Neuropsychology. His service to the profession and to society has been recognized as well through the President's Gold Medal for Service to the National Academy of Neuropsychology as well as the Academy's Distinguished Service Award, and the University of North Carolina at Wilmington's 50th Anniversary Razor Walker Award for Service to the Youth of North Carolina. He is currently a Professor of Educational Psychology, Professor of Neuroscience, and Distinguished Research Scholar at Texas A&M University.